This book is about winning;
how to win in combat and how to win in life.
Read it carefully, apply the strategies,
and you too will be a winner.

THE SECRET SCIENCE OF COMBAT STRATEGY

By Jules Aib

FOUNDER OF WORLD AIKIDO-YOGA

www.worldaikidoyoga.com
www.myedojo.com

Balboa Press books may be ordered through booksellers or by contacting:

Balboa Press
A Division of Hay House
1663 Liberty Drive
Bloomington, IN 47403
www.balboapress.com.au
1-(877) 407-4847

ISBN: 978-1-4525-0723-1 (sc)
ISBN: 978-1-4525-0724-8 (e)

Printed in the United States of America

Balboa Press rev. date: 10/26/2012

Please note: By downloading this book as an e-book or obtaining a hardcopy version of this book, you declare that you have read, understood, and accepted the Release of Liability Waiver, Medical Disclaimer, and General Content disclaimer published.

Release of Liability Waiver

By downloading this book as an e-book or by obtaining a hardcopy version of this book you intend to be legally bound and do hereby agree to be legally bound for yourself and for all successors in interest you may have, by this Release of Liability Waiver, and hereby agree to hold harmless and indemnify World Aikido-Yoga (WAY), WAY crew, as well as any officers, members, employees, assistants, volunteers, assigns, or agents of any type whatsoever acting on or in behalf of the aforementioned entities and persons, against any claims for damages or other claims for injuries or losses of any kind suffered by you or any others, directly or indirectly, arising out of any practice, instructions, or other activity related to *The Secret Science of Combat Strategy*. By downloading this book as an e-book or by obtaining a hardcopy version you understand that the combat strategies are to be used at your own risk, that the aforementioned trainers, personnel, and businesses assume no responsibility for your actions should you attempt to use any of these skills, methods, or exercises. By downloading this book as an e-book or by obtaining a hardcopy version you understand that the secret strategies of combat science involve potentially hazardous activities and conditions, and you further understand that the practice of any combat strategy will require you to be in good physical condition. By downloading this book as an e-book or by obtaining a hardcopy version you certify that you are physically able to participate in this activity and will further hold World Aikido-Yoga (WAY), W.A.Y crew, as well as any officers, members, employees, assistants, volunteers, assigns, or agents of any type whatsoever acting on or in behalf of the aforementioned entities and persons, harmless for any injury sustained in the course of your combat strategy training due to any physical defect or condition that you may have, whether now known or hereinafter discovered. By downloading this book as an e-book or by obtaining a hardcopy version you further acknowledge that this release shall not expire and shall be considered effective in perpetuity. You, therefore, fully accept the risk associated with martial arts training, and understand the risks associated with following any instruction related to martial arts training. By downloading this book as an e-book or by obtaining a hardcopy version you have understood *all* that is expressed in this text above, and you certify that you are of sound judgment and legally competent to agree to this Release of Liability Waiver.

Medical Disclaimer

Consult your doctor before attempting any exercise device or program. Do not use if you have any special medical condition. Only your doctor or a qualified medical professional can provide you with advice or recommendations for an individual ailment, treatment, or problem. Martial-arts training is dangerous. Train at your own risk.

General Content

All the information in this book is meant exclusively for educational and informational purposes. By downloading this book as an e-book or by obtaining a hardcopy version you are subject to these terms and conditions. By downloading this book as an e-book or obtaining a hardcopy version, you accept, without limitation or qualification, these terms.

Any party engaging in illegal activities involving the use of this book will be subject to civil and criminal prosecution. All information contained within this book is only available to persons who are over the age of eighteen and are legally allowed to enter binding contracts. World Aikido-Yoga (WAY) cannot guarantee that it will notice or be able to prevent any illegal or inappropriate use of this material, nor can World Aikido-Yoga (WAY) guarantee that it will give notice of any illegal or inappropriate use of this book. The information is believed to be accurate and current at the time the information was presented in this book. World Aikido-Yoga (WAY) and/or its respective suppliers and publishers or schools make no representations about the suitability of the information contained in this document and related graphics published for any purpose. The content and related graphics published in this book may include technical inaccuracies or typographical errors. Changes are periodically made to the information herein. World Aikido-Yoga (WAY) and/or its respective suppliers and publishers may make improvements and changes to the content or the program(s) described herein at any time without prior notice.

In no event shall World Aikido-Yoga (WAY) or its respective suppliers and publishers or affiliates be liable for any special, indirect, or consequential damages or any damages whatsoever resulting from loss of use, data, or profits, whether in an action of contract, negligence, or other tortuous action, arising out of or in connection with the use or performance of material, documents, provision of, or failure to provide services or information available from this book.

None of World Aikido-Yoga (WAY), its related bodies corporate, any of their directors, officers or employees, affiliates, related companies, or its licensees, or joint-project partners, make any representation or warranty as to the reliability, accuracy, or completeness of the information contained in this book (including in relation to any products or services) and none of them accept any responsibility arising in any way (including negligence) for errors in, or omissions from, the information contained in this book. World Aikido-Yoga (WAY) disclaims all representations and warranties, express or implied, including but not limited to, implied warranties of merchantability and fitness for a particular purpose and noninfringement to the fullest extent permitted by applicable law. World Aikido-Yoga (WAY) makes no warranty that this book or any products or services described within this book will be timely, secure, errorless, uninterrupted, or meet any specific requirements you may have. No advice, suggestion, or information, whether printed, oral, or written, obtained by you from or through this book creates any warranty not expressly made in these Terms and Conditions.

Information in this book pertaining to products and/or services has been prepared in accordance with Australian laws only. This information may not satisfy the laws of some other country. In case these Terms and Conditions do not satisfy the laws of the country in which you reside or from which you are accessing this book, this book and its content are not meant for your use and cannot be relied upon by you, and you may not use it. If you choose to use this book, you agree to indemnify World Aikido-Yoga (WAY) against any losses, costs, expenses, or damages.

You expressly acknowledge and agree that you understand that World Aikido-Yoga (WAY) does not possess control over other users of this book or the suppliers and publishers of goods and services from World Aikido-Yoga (WAY). Thus World Aikido-Yoga (WAY) is, therefore, not liable for their opinions, their behavior, or their acts, including any information or advice provided by them or any defamatory statements made by them or any offensive conduct on their part.

Testimonials

- "*Martial-arts* has given me a direction to where I want to be. It inspires and challenges me physically, mentally, and spiritually. The only way to understand this is to experience it for yourself."—**Dr. Mirella Dottori, stem cell research scientist**

- "The time I spend training in *martial-arts* is an investment that compounds into every area of my life."—**Mr. Daniel Sharp, teacher**

- "Amazing! There's no end in sight. Each step I am guided on leads me to secret, hidden places I never could have imagined existed."—**Mr. Daniel Somerville, IT consultant**

- "*Martial-arts* is about growing into a better version of myself. I am certainly a different person—a calmer, more focused, and healthier person—because of my training." —**Mr. James Irving, lawyer**

- "*Budō* has started a journey of self-discovery within me that has offered me more than any book I've ever read. It has a special way of showing the beauty of art and life. As an artist, I realise that there are no tricks, just a constant testing of the body. However *Aikido-Yoga* is showing me how to move beyond the body in pursuit of a better understanding of myself and my art."—**Mr. Kieran Gourley, dancer, Australian Ballet Company**

- "When I first decided to look for a *dojo* to train in a marital art I trolled the Internet and other resources trying to find a style that would suit my needs. I had a very specific set of criteria. Searching high and low, I was looking for a way to gain effective life skills in addition to increase my flexibility, as well as something that was both physically and mentally challenging. Somewhere I could grow. There were so many martial-art styles to choose from, and so I studied the advantages and disadvantages of every form. I'd done and excelled in many other sports and skills that only left me wanting more. When I came across Aikido-Yoga, it struck me as being something very different to the other martial arts on offer. It came across as not just a pastime or a recreational sport to win a few trophies, but more of a type of lifestyle. It appeared to meet my criteria, and had a more holistic approach to the human condition that I found very appealing—stimulating mind, body, and soul without overly feeding my ego with the more competitive, aggressive, tactile gratification approaches endorsed by so many other martial arts.

When researching Aikido, I found a surprising amount of older and even very old people that were still actively practicing with a certain sense of youthful vigour and movement. Free flowing with seemingly no resistance, they would overcome much younger and fitter opponents. This really struck a chord with me as I contemplated what other martial art could offer me the ability to effectively perform even in my latter years. At this point I hadn't had any experience with yoga and often wondered what all the hype was about. So, I decided to go and see what it was all about.

The first time I went to the *dojo* was an overwhelming experience. A whole new world existed without my knowledge. For the first time in my life I truly felt way out of my depth and really challenged from day one. Upon speaking to other people, some of whom had been training there for more than four years, I learnt that they still had the same feeling of constantly being challenged. There was a certain unexplainable vibe coming from the *dojo*, and the people within it, a very calm but alert place where time seemed to stand still. I remember thinking after the first few lessons how quickly they had passed. Two years on and they still pass in a "blink of an eye." It's only in reflection after class, when journaling my experiences that the true value of the learning actually starts to sink in. The original expectations and set criteria from when I first went to the *dojo* have vastly changed. Aikido-Yoga really is a *way* of life. The principles I learn here can be applied to every aspect of my life. It has undoubtedly changed me for the better, and will continue to do so well into my senior years."—**Darren Horkings, business consultant**

Jules Aib

Founder of World Aikido-Yoga (WAY)

CONTENTS

The Secret Science of Combat Strategy

Contents continued . . .

Contents continued . . .

END

"Let us train our mind to desire
what the situation demands."

—Seneca

The Secret Science of Combat Strategy

Prelude

Because you have found your way to this book, it is possible that you are ready to progress beyond the mere study of technique, in whatever martial discipline you have chosen to practise, and move into the realm of martial *art*.

Within these pages you will begin to delve into the mystical and mysterious path of budō, starting with the secret science of combat strategy elevated to an art form.

Please feel free to take from this book anything you consider of value. Also feel free to discard anything you consider of no use to you at this stage of your training.

> ***"The beginning of knowledge is the discovery of something we do not understand."***
>
> *—Frank Herbert*

"Look at every path closely and deliberately.
Try it as many times as you think necessary.
Then ask yourself, and yourself alone, one question.
This question is one that only a very old man asks.
My benefactor told me about it once when I was young,
And my blood was too vigorous for me to understand it.
Now I do understand it.
I will tell you what it is: does this path have a heart?
All paths are the same: they lead nowhere.
They are paths going through the bush, or into the bush.
In my own life I could say I have traversed long, long paths,
But I am not anywhere.
My benefactor's question has meaning now.
Does this path have a heart?
If it does, the path is good; if it doesn't, it is of no use.
Both paths lead nowhere; but one has a heart, the other doesn't.
One makes for a joyful journey;
as long as you follow it, you are one with it.
The other will make you curse your life.
One makes you strong; the other weakens you."

—Carlos Castaneda, *Teachings of Don Juan*

Does Your Path Have a Heart?

As a beginner you naturally started trying to mimic the technical aspects of your chosen martial art by copying the form and structure of the physical techniques. For years you may have operated only at this superficial periphery of your discipline: its outward appearance. This is understandable because most teachers are capable only of demonstrating the outer shell of their art; they have not yet attained a level where they can begin to transmit its heart.

Therefore, for you to become a true martial artist, you need to be led much deeper—right into your art's essence, directly into its heart. From there, you can naturally allow the outward appearance of the art form to reveal itself to you. Each person must accomplish this for himself or herself. You can only be shown the entrance to the door. From that point on, your sustained effort is required to pass through and see for yourself what's on the other side.

For you to be able to pass through that door you must begin to allow yourself to feel, to experience, and then to simply witness events as they unfold moment by moment. Your reality will no longer be diluted by what you think has happened, should happen, is happening, or will happen based on any number of filters and distortions that your mind has built up over a lifetime of adverse experience and conditioning.

At this point in your training, you will then be ready to move beyond form. You will begin to understand not so much based on what you have been taught but based on what you are able to intuit. It is like glimpsing someone familiar on the other side of a large, crowded room only to realise that you are looking at yourself in a distant mirror; you are still the same person, but everything is different because your interpretation of what your senses are telling you has changed. Your understanding of reality is different. You now see into the heart of things, past their surface appearance, past their form into the commonality of all things. You may even feel a little embarrassed that you did not recognise this reality, in all its simple elegance, sooner, because it was there all along, hidden in plain sight.

"Just as you see yourself in a mirror,
form and reflection look at each other.
You are not the reflection, yet the reflection is you."

—Tosan

Because your stable, centred internal state can no longer be unsettled by information that you now understand does not reflect reality, you are free to remain present, with no distraction of mind that might disconnect you from your positive, purposeful actions. Although respectful of other people's beliefs, you personally do not pay much heed to intellectual interpretations, religious discussions, or theosophical debates, nor do you give any credence to any esoteric belief systems, philosophies, or teachings. Simply and quietly, without ego or distraction, fuelled by curiosity and wonder, with your faculties of reason and discernment fully engaged, you simply continue to train as before, without distraction.

This kind of egoless, centred training prepares you as much for death as it does for life because, as the present moment expands to become your natural state of being, you gradually lose all fear of death. Irrational fear, like dogged belief systems, coexists with ignorance and a lack of true understanding. Darkness is simply the absence of light, and no darkness can possibly exist in the light of your newfound understanding. With all illusion dissolved, you now make choices and take actions to free yourself from fear, guilt, obligation, or shame. This hard-fought freedom is a major milestone on your personal journey to merge completely with the very heart of your art form. The effort required to accomplish this level of awareness is considerable. The reward for such effort is life in abundance.

***"Does your path have a heart?
If it doesn't, it is of no use."***

—Carlos Castaneda, *Teachings of Don Juan*

"Just as you see yourself in a mirror,
form and reflection look at each other.
You are not the reflection,
yet the reflection is you."

—Tosan

Why Do You Need a Strategy?

In sport combat, the ultimate objective is to win each contest. Luck, good technical ability, and individual effort may be major factors in any victory, but to string together a succession of significant accomplishments over a lifetime requires a strategy and strong allies.

In life, the ultimate objective is not only to survive but also to live joyfully for many years. Either way, to keep accomplishing your goals, you must effectively build a strong support base of people who are also getting their objectives met by helping you.

"True victory is self-victory."

—Morihei Ueshiba

True combat strategy requires that you first and foremost know yourself and then all the external factors that may have a bearing on your desired outcome. Skilful introspection must therefore always precede a careful study of the external factors that may influence success or defeat. Correct insight must not be based only on accurate intelligence gathering but must also encompass a detailed knowledge of all the mental, emotional, psychological, and subconscious factors that may have an influence on your desired outcome.

Long-term, effective actions are always based in reality, not guesswork. Your approach, therefore, cannot be haphazard;

it must be based in science. A scientific approach naturally implies a continuous, never-ending cycle of study, application, experimentation, and rethinking. Just like science, strategy requires imagination and also that you allow room for spontaneous improvisation and insight. If your strategy lacks these essential ingredients then even though you may have some success, your actions will not survive the test of time because you will become ineffective when confronted with evolving circumstance. In this way, the application of creative imagination and spontaneous improvisation elevates the science of strategy to an art form.

The secret combat strategies articulated in this book are grounded in fundamental principles and are, therefore, universally applicable and equally effective irrespective of the specific fighting method or techniques employed. They also are by their nature universally applicable to armed as well as to unarmed interactions. In addition, these strategies are equally applicable to sport combat as well as to real life-and-death encounters because, unlike techniques, strategies and principles are not restricted by rules. Like techniques, however, principles and strategies need to be correctly understood and applied repeatedly until they become second nature.

"There exists no measure of time fast or slow.
It is not a question of speed.
The technique is over before it is begun."

—*Morihei Ueshiba*

TREE METAPHOR

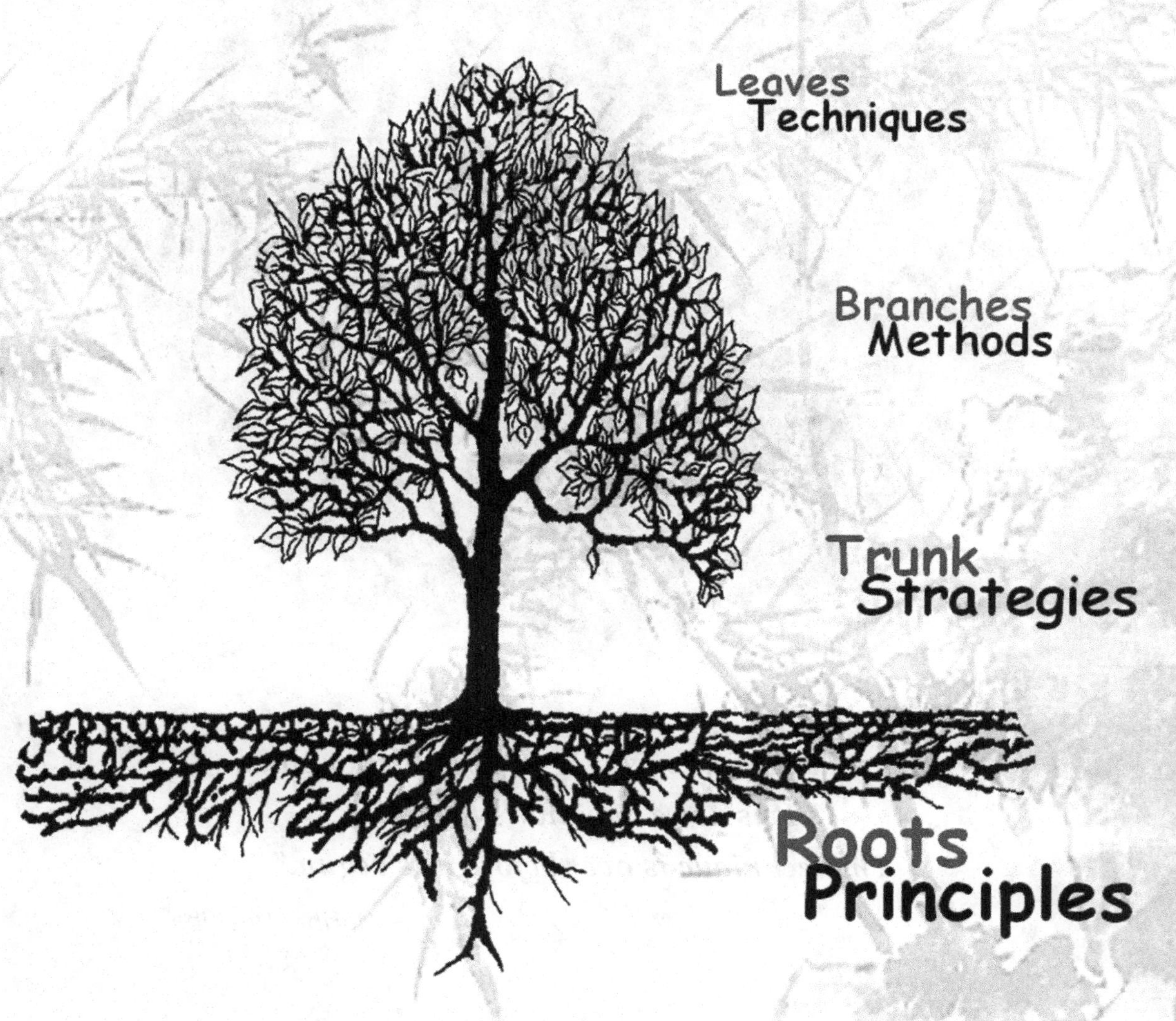

Figure 1: Tree Metaphor

Tree Metaphor

Like a tree, to survive harsh and unforgiving situations, you need to be flexible yet remain stable, grounded, deep-rooted, centred, and strong. Ultimately, your goal is to grow in all aspects of your life and contribute to the world in meaningful ways that align your actions to your true purpose. This is a very important and practical aspect of training in budō and yoga.

- To start, you need to surround yourself with talented, positive, and supportive people. Immersing yourself into a nurturing environment (i.e., ensuring the tree is planted in good soil) is essential to developing to your full potential.

- The effectiveness of the countless number of techniques (the leaves of the tree) that you can perform from the numerous armed and unarmed combat methods (the tree branches) depends on the effectiveness of the strategies (the tree trunk) and the fundamental principles (the tree roots) that underpin every combat method or system you employ.

- The many leaves of the tree continue to spontaneously change and adapt as the many branches of the tree sway and adapt as appropriate to the many unique, unpredictable, volatile, and ever-changing circumstances you face.

- It doesn't matter how many times the wind changes direction or how hard it rains, the trunk of the tree, supported by the tree's roots, remains stable to sustain the creative process of the branches and the leaves.

- If the tree remains stable, strong, and centred, then it will continue to rejuvenate, naturally produce seeds or fruit (positive, practical, measurable outcomes; results), realise its full potential, and fulfil its life's purpose.

- In time, the life-affirming, spiritual, and esoteric forces of nature will naturally give rise to new life.

"Life itself is always a trial. In training, you must test and polish yourself to face the great challenges of life. Transcend the realm of life and death, and then you will be able to make your way calmly and safely through any crisis that confronts you."

—Morihei Ueshiba

The MyeDōjō
Five Curriculum Levels
Five Levels of Progression

The *MyeDōjō*

The Japanese term ***dōjō*** literally translates as *"way-place"* or a place where you follow a *path* or *way to illumination/clarity*. It is where you go for personal transformation. As such a *dōjō* is a place where everyone is committed to being part of a community that is dedicated to helping each other with their personal endeavour to merge completely with the *very heart* of their chosen art form.

Within this global community, made possible with the advent of the Internet, you are presented with a unique opportunity to join a virtual *dōjō*—without walls and without limitations. World Aikido-Yoga (WAY) is pioneering the development of a unique *MyeDōjō*, which offers online access to live classes, workshops, and seminars grouped within five distinct certification levels, which are subsequently archived for unlimited future reference by *MyeDōjō* members.

The course of instruction offered within the online *MyeDōjō* training sessions walks you through, step by step, a series of practical exercises and drills that will help you to master not only the combat strategies outlined in this book, but also give you the full spectrum of instruction from basic combat techniques all the way through to the most advanced theory and practical application of both combat and yoga techniques, strategies, and principles available anywhere.

As with any traditional *dōjō,* based on a comprehensive training and accreditation process, you will gain the proficiency required for advancement through each of the five major certification levels. This will enable you to practice solo or with others in the comfort of your own home or *dōjō* using the structured real-time, online classes as well as the extensive and ever-growing online video archive reference library.

True martial-arts practice is multifaceted in order to enhance every aspect of your life. The lessons learnt within the five major certification levels of *MyeDōjō,* therefore, enable you to interpret the secret wisdom contained within *Budō* and *Yoga* and translate this ancient knowledge into practical application in everyday, real-life situations when it counts the most—under pressure.

> ***"Your eventual goal is to become a simple, compassionate, free-thinking individual without badge or title, living a life of true authenticity and integrity."***
>
> —*Jules Aib*

The MyeDōjō
Five Curriculum Levels
Five Levels of Progression

The Five MyeDōjō Curriculum Levels

Level 1: Combat Methods and Techniques

[The "branches" and "leaves" depicted in the tree metaphor.]

This level of training gives you access to a comprehensive curriculum of very sophisticated martial-*arts forms and techniques*. These consist of numerous empty-hand and grappling techniques as well as a full array of traditional weapons instruction. The level of instruction you will receive in the *MyeDōjō* has previously only been available to people who have had the opportunity to receive in-depth one-on-one training with an advanced instructor who was able to impart a deeper understanding of martial-arts techniques.

Level 2: Combat Strategies

[The "trunk" depicted in the tree metaphor.]

This level of training gives you access to an in-depth study of the theory and practical application of the secret science of *combat strategy*. This covers empty-hand, grappling as well as traditional weapons practice. The level of instruction you will receive in the *MyeDōjō* has previously only been available to people who have had the opportunity to receive in-depth one-on-one training with an advanced instructor who was able to impart a deeper understanding of martial arts combat strategies.

Level 3: Combat Principles

[The "roots" depicted in the tree metaphor.]

This level of training gives you access to a detailed explanation and an in-depth study of the fundamental *principles* that underpin the practice and application of martial strategies, methods, and techniques. This covers empty-hand and grappling as well as traditional weapons practice. The level of instruction you will receive in the *MyeDōjō* has previously only been available to people who have had the opportunity to receive in-depth one-on-one training with an advanced instructor who was able to impart a deeper understanding of martial-arts principles.

Level 4: Personal Growth

[How tall does a tree grow? As tall as it can!]

This level of training gives you access to a comprehensive and ever evolving set of *personal growth* tools, strategies, and principles that will facilitate your personal growth and support the attainment of your life goals. The level of instruction you will receive in the *MyeDōjō* has previously only been available to people who have had the opportunity to receive in-depth one-on-one training with an advanced instructor who was able, or even willing, to impart to you a deeper understanding of the more practical, noncombat aspects of your training as they apply to your life purpose based on your aptitude and dedication.

Level 5: Expanding Awareness

[Beyond the self . . .]

This level of training gives you access to an in-depth study of the more *esoteric/spiritual aspects* of *Budō* and *Yoga* that will breathe new life and vitality into your martial-arts practice. This encompasses empty-hand as well as traditional weapons practice. The level of instruction you will receive in the *MyeDōjō* has previously only been available to people who have had the opportunity to receive in-depth one-on-one training with an advanced instructor who was able, or even willing, to impart a deeper understanding of the more esoteric/spiritual aspects of martial arts based on your aptitude and dedication.

"True martial-arts practice is multifaceted to enhance every aspect of your life"

—Jules Aib

The MyeDōjō
Five Curriculum Levels
Five Levels of Progression

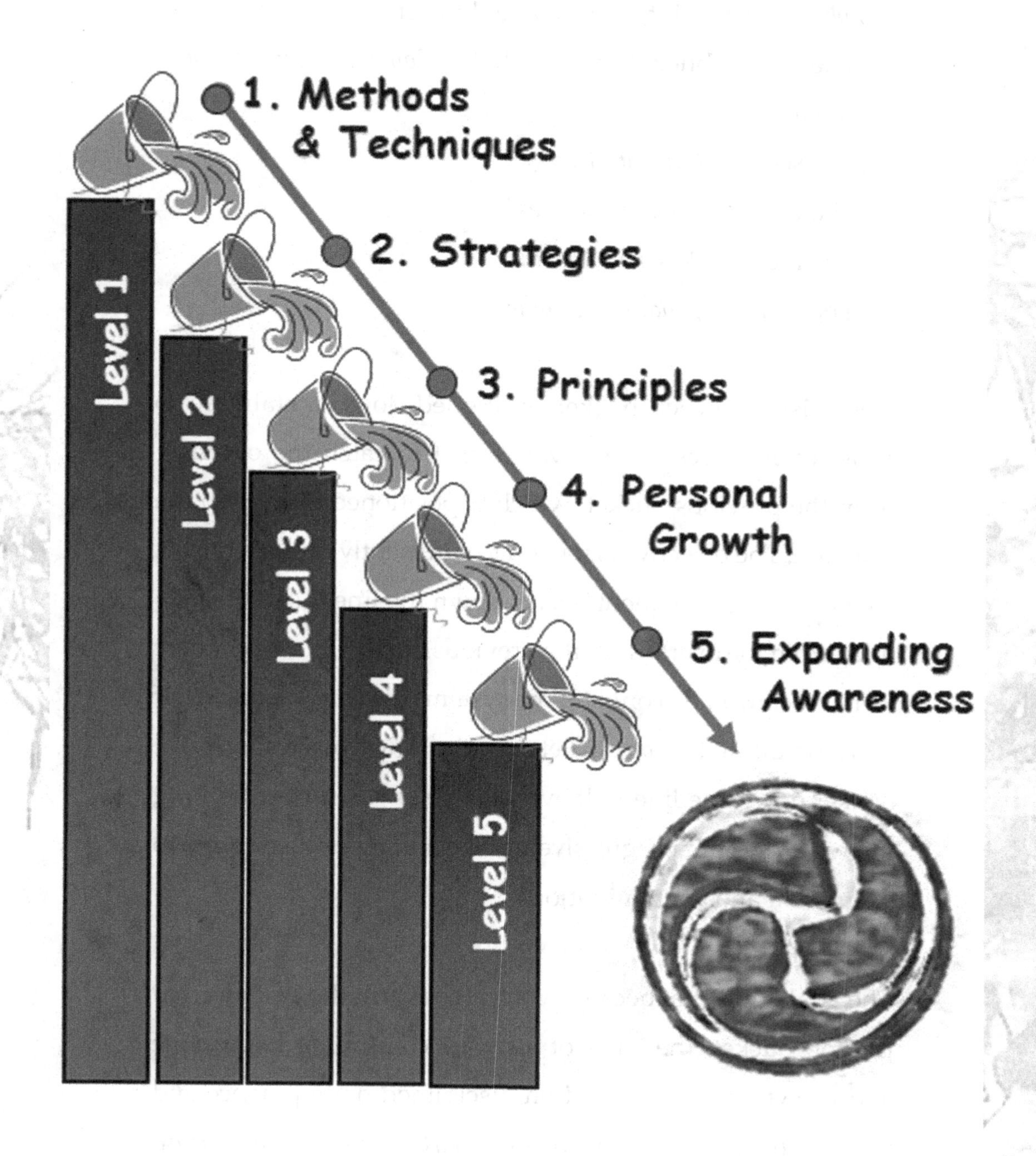

Figure 2: Learning Sequence

The Five Levels of Progression

Imagine apportioning the contents of one large bucket called *"Combat Mastery"* into five smaller buckets:

- The first bucket you label *"Combat Methods and Techniques"*
- The second *"Combat Strategies"*
- The third *"Combat Principles"*
- The fourth *"Personal Growth"*
- The fifth *"Expanding Awareness"*

Now visualise each bucket positioned down a staircase to allow each successively lower bucket to catch the overflow from the previous bucket, which is positioned higher up the staircase. The objective is for you to sufficiently fill each bucket so that every subsequent bucket down the line is successively filled from the overflow of the previous bucket. However, there is the catch; you can only fill the system from the top bucket. If you stop filling the *top* bucket then the flow to each successive bucket down the line will eventually slow to a stop, making the whole system progressively more and more susceptible to stagnation and contamination.

The analogy is that because you can only fill the system from the top bucket, the basis of all your continuing knowledge and growth must be based on disciplined daily practice and refinement of *technique* in whatever *martial combat method(s)* you choose. Progressive mastery of ***techniques*** within a variety of ***combat methods*** *(bucket 1)* therefore allows you to apply more skilful application of ***strategy*** *(bucket 2),* which in turn enables you to better understand and apply the fundamental ***principles*** *(bucket 3)* that underpin all the combat methods and techniques. As the process of learning pegs new knowledge to previous understanding, you will naturally start to relate the lessons you learn in the *MyeDōjō* to your everyday life experiences in a continuous cycle of ***personal growth*** *(bucket 4).* This lays the foundation for ***expanding awareness*** *(bucket 5),* resulting in a gradual blossoming of your wisdom and esoteric/spiritual insight.

If you do not approach your training in the above sequential manner and instead try to fill the buckets in the wrong order, then, at best, you will have an incomplete approach, and at worst, you will be faced with a potentially ineffective system that is susceptible to dogma and stagnation. Regardless of whether your objective is combat mastery, personal development, or spiritual growth, if your practice is based solely on a theoretical, mental, or faith-based approach, and not on disciplined daily physical practice that reinforces a personal journey of self-discovery, then you are essentially wasting your time because you need all of the successive buckets overflowing in sequence in order for you to attain any level of real mastery that can survive real-life pressure.

More importantly, your mind/body experience resulting from physical practice will enable the overflow of gratitude, compassion, and love from the last bucket to fill your heart. *Eventually, your heart will also naturally start to overflow.* This is the source of all true *self-full* contribution. Fear and love cannot live in the same heart at the same time, so as all your fear is displaced with love, the resulting overflow of love from your heart will result in the emergence of a truly courageous and authentic spirit that is ready, willing, and able to contribute to the world in ways that are congruent with your life purpose. The overflow of the last bucket in the sequential chain is therefore a key milestone along your martial-arts journey.

However, regardless of your chosen martial discipline, your journey must start with your body—from the daily study and practice of the *techniques* related to your chosen *martial method(s)/system(s)* (bucket 1). The eventual overflow of unconditional, boundless love and compassion from your heart, and your ensuing self-full contribution, will accelerate your inevitable journey along your chosen martial path back to the Absolute.

Combat Strategies
1.0
Combat Distance
2.0
Combat Timing
3.0
Combat Momentum
4.0
Control of Centre
5.0
Pre-empting
6.0
Pre-combat

The Combat Strategies

As stated in the opening paragraph of this book, you are about to be introduced to *the secret science of combat strategy—elevated to an art form.*

What you are about to learn are not tricks, or specific things that, if you do them in the right sequence and in the correct manner will magically deliver you the victory you so strongly desire. In fact this very desire of yours will drive your goal of successful combat strategy ever further from your grasp in direct proportion to your strong desire!

"It responds with versatile facility,
But its function cannot be located.
Therefore when you look for it,
You become further from it,
When you seek it,
You turn away from it all the more."

—Linji

What you are about to be presented with is a new way of thinking and a new way of being in which each strategy and principle introduced is capable of being physically tested—*under pressure*—in order for you to be able to experiment with and verify the results for yourself.

The scientific nature of the practice method will give you immediate tangible feedback that will instantly let you know where you need to make adjustments to the application of the particular combat strategy you are attempting to perfect. If you try a specific combat strategy, and it does not work for you, then you will receive instant feedback that will enable you to suitably modify your approach or switch to another strategy that may be more suitable for you.

Like considering the various aspects of the tree metaphor, the following defined strategies can be studied in isolation; however, in practical application they all merge and overlap in interdependent ways that blur the clearly defined edges of each articulated strategy into a holistic way of being and interacting with your opponents that will give you new insight into the meaning behind the expression *"all is one."*

"It is necessary to develop a strategy
that utilizes all the physical conditions
and elements that are directly at hand.
The best strategy relies upon an
unlimited set of responses."

—Morihei Ueshiba

A VERY IMPORTANT NOTE PRIOR TO THE STUDY OF COMBAT STRATEGY

A very important requirement: The practical application of any combat strategy is predicated with the requirement that you have previously mastered—*to a certain degree*—the physical techniques, forms, and variations of the specific combat method you are employing, be it either an empty-hand or a weapons-based system. You must be a proficient technician prior to attempting to employ a strategy. This rule applies equally and uniformly across all professions, whether it is a doctor, lawyer, plumber, or martial artist. You must first hone your technique before considering strategy.

The combat strategies articulated in this book will therefore support your progress if you are already proficient in a specific set of martial-arts techniques or are currently heavily into mixed martial-arts (MMA) training. However, regardless of the discipline you have chosen, you must have attained a certain level of technical proficiency in order to move on to the study of combat strategy. You cannot easily and free-flowingly apply yourself to the study of strategy if you are trying to remember footwork or cannot apply the techniques with a certain level of technical proficiency. If you are *not* already technically proficient in a martial art then your understanding and subsequent application of combat strategy will be significantly lacking. If you are already a good technician in your chosen martial-arts discipline or are an advanced practitioner of mixed martial arts, then away you go; enjoy the practice of *the secret science of combat strategy!*

The course of instruction offered to you within the online *MyeDōjō* training sessions will further walk you through, step by step, a series of practical exercises and drills that will help you to master the following combat strategies, which you can then readily apply to your chosen martial-art form.

The combat strategies summarised in this book constitute the second level of training in the five-step online *MyeDōjō* curriculum. If you are not yet proficient in a specific set of techniques from your chosen martial discipline, then I suggest that you start from the first course of *MyeDōjō* instruction—*Combat Methods and Techniques.*

***MyeDōjō* Curriculum Levels:**

- ***Level 1:*** *Combat Methods and Techniques*
- ***Level 2:*** ***Combat Strategy***
- ***Level 3:*** *Combat Principles*
- ***Level 4:*** *Personal Growth*
- ***Level 5:*** *Expanding Awareness*

COMBAT STRATEGY

"Even though our path is completely different from the warrior arts of the past, it is not necessary to abandon totally the old ways. Absorb venerable traditions into this Art by clothing them with fresh garments, and building on the classic styles to create better forms"

—*Morihei Ueshiba*

Combat Strategies
1.0
Combat Distance
2.0
Combat Timing
3.0
Combat Momentum
4.0
Control of Centre
5.0
Pre-empting
6.0
Pre-combat

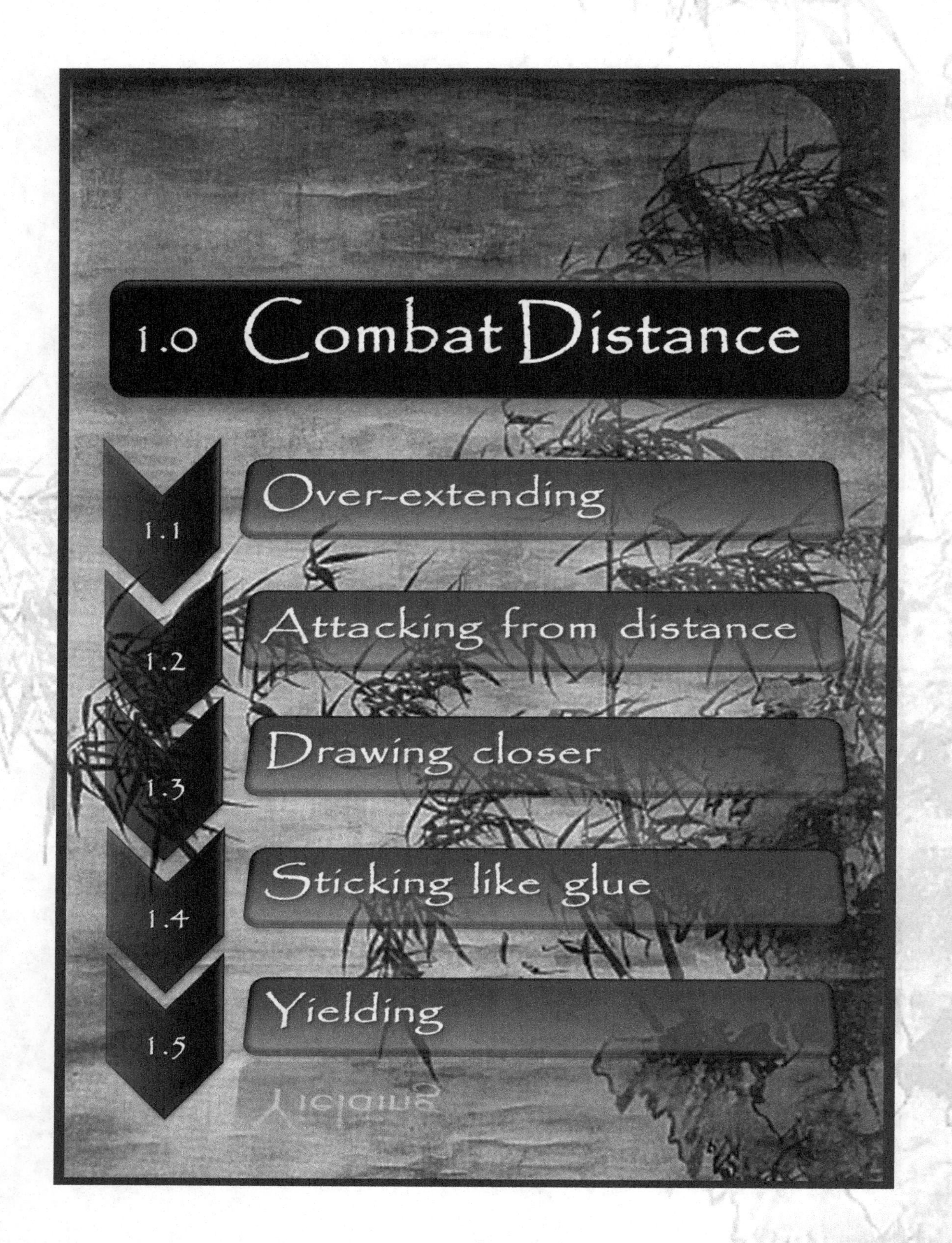
1.0 Combat Distance
1.1
Over-extending
1.2
Attacking from distance
1.3
Drawing closer
1.4
Sticking like glue
1.5
Yielding

1.0 Combat Distance Strategy

Combat distance is one of the most important things you must consider and something that you must learn how to constantly manipulate to your advantage. Careful consideration must also be given to the numerous factors that could influence correct combat distance *(e.g., terrain, lighting, surrounding objects, weapons vs. empty-hand distance, etc.)*

With practice *(especially once you start to incorporate rhythm and timing exercises),* your ability to evade strikes by millimetres instead of centimetres will dramatically improve the timing and effectiveness of your counterattacks.

The first basic rule that defines *optimum combat distance* is that your opponent must take one step forward to execute any technique against you. It is also the best distance from which you can deliver a strike that incorporates forward momentum and the maximum use of your bodyweight to increase the effectiveness of your strike. Any distance *beyond* this circumference is well outside of the appropriate range to deliver a decisive attack. Any distance *within* this circumference is well within the range to make contact without the need to take an advancing step. This *optimum combat distance* also varies depending on your or your opponent's level of athleticism.

Much practice is required in order to correctly gauge the exact maximum effective range of either empty-hand or weapons strikes while taking into consideration the numerous factors that influence correct combat distance *(e.g., environment, type of weapon, size and athleticism of the opponent, etc.)*

Another important consideration when you study optimal striking range is your minimum effective striking range. The minimum effective striking range is the distance from which you can no longer deliver a decisive blow. Once the minimum effective striking range has been encountered, grappling techniques may be a much more effective way for you to gain advantage or improve your position.

The course of instruction offered to you within the online *MyeDōjō* training sessions will further walk you through, step by step, a series of practical exercises and drills that will help you to master the following combat distance strategies.

"Techniques employ four qualities that reflect the nature of our world. Depending on the circumstance, you should be: hard as a diamond, flexible as a willow, smooth-flowing like water, or empty as space."

—Morihei Ueshiba

1.0 Combat Distance
1.1
Over-extending
1.2
Attacking from distance
1.3
Drawing closer
1.4
Sticking like glue
1.5
Yielding

1.1 Overextending

As noted in the previous chapter, the *optimal combat distance* is where your opponent must take one step forward to execute any technique against you. The specific combat distance strategy reviewed in this chapter involves your ability to get your opponent to slightly overextend his or her strike when he or she attempts to launch an attack against you from a distance *slightly farther away* from you than what you consider to be *his or her* optimal combat distance *(i.e., where your opponent must take more than one step forward to execute any technique against you).*

In order to pull this strategy off you need to carefully manoeuvre yourself to a distance *only* one or so centimetres beyond what you consider to be *your opponent's* optimum combat distance *(i.e., where your opponent must take slightly more than one step forward to execute any technique against you.)*

The next part of this strategy is to either somehow encourage your opponent to launch an attack from this suboptimal distance or simply take advantage of the opportunity if it presents itself. Consequently the attack will either be slightly overextended or, at worst, he or she will have had to make a slight position adjustment to get to the optimum combat distance prior to launching the attack. This will give you ample warning to immediately readjust your position. If the distance you create is greater than a centimetre or so over the optimum combat distance from your opponent, then it will be very difficult for you to get an experienced opponent to initiate an attack.

There are many creative ways you can experiment with to create this slight distance buffer yet present the illusion of an optimal combat distance to your opponent. One simple way is, while both of you are manoeuvring into position, when you adjust your position relative to your opponent you move your feet to a position that places you one or so centimetres past your opponent's optimum combat distance while projecting your torso to appear to be at your opponent's optimum combat distance. As soon as your opponent launches an attack you simply adjust your torso back slightly into balance and take advantage of his or her now slightly overextended/off-posture attack. Another way for you to draw out his or her attack at this extended distance would be to feint a movement, adopt an aggressive expression, look away slightly as if distracted, or even breathe in a way that might entice them to attack you while at this slightly suboptimal combat distance. But remember, if the gap you create is too large, then your opponent will either have an opportunity to disengage or to shuffle in quick enough to regain his or her balance and launch an attack from correct combat distance.

Use your imagination. Experiment with and improvise many new ways to create this ever-so-slight buffer to take advantage of your opponent's overextended attack. The options to create as well as to take advantage of this opportunity are only limited by your imagination and ingenuity. This strategy works equally well for striking, grappling, and weapons-based arts. The trick is to remain calm, to keep it subtle, and to not be too obvious or try too hard to overextend your opponent's attack. Over time, you will recognise many new ways to creatively take advantage of the opportunities presented by this strategy.

The course of instruction offered to you within the online *MyeDōjō* training sessions will further walk you through, step by step, a series of practical exercises and drills that will help you to master the above combat distance strategy, which you can then readily apply to your chosen martial-art form.

"Even the most powerful human being has a limited sphere of strength. Draw him outside of that sphere and into your own, and his strength will dissipate"

—Morihei Ueshiba

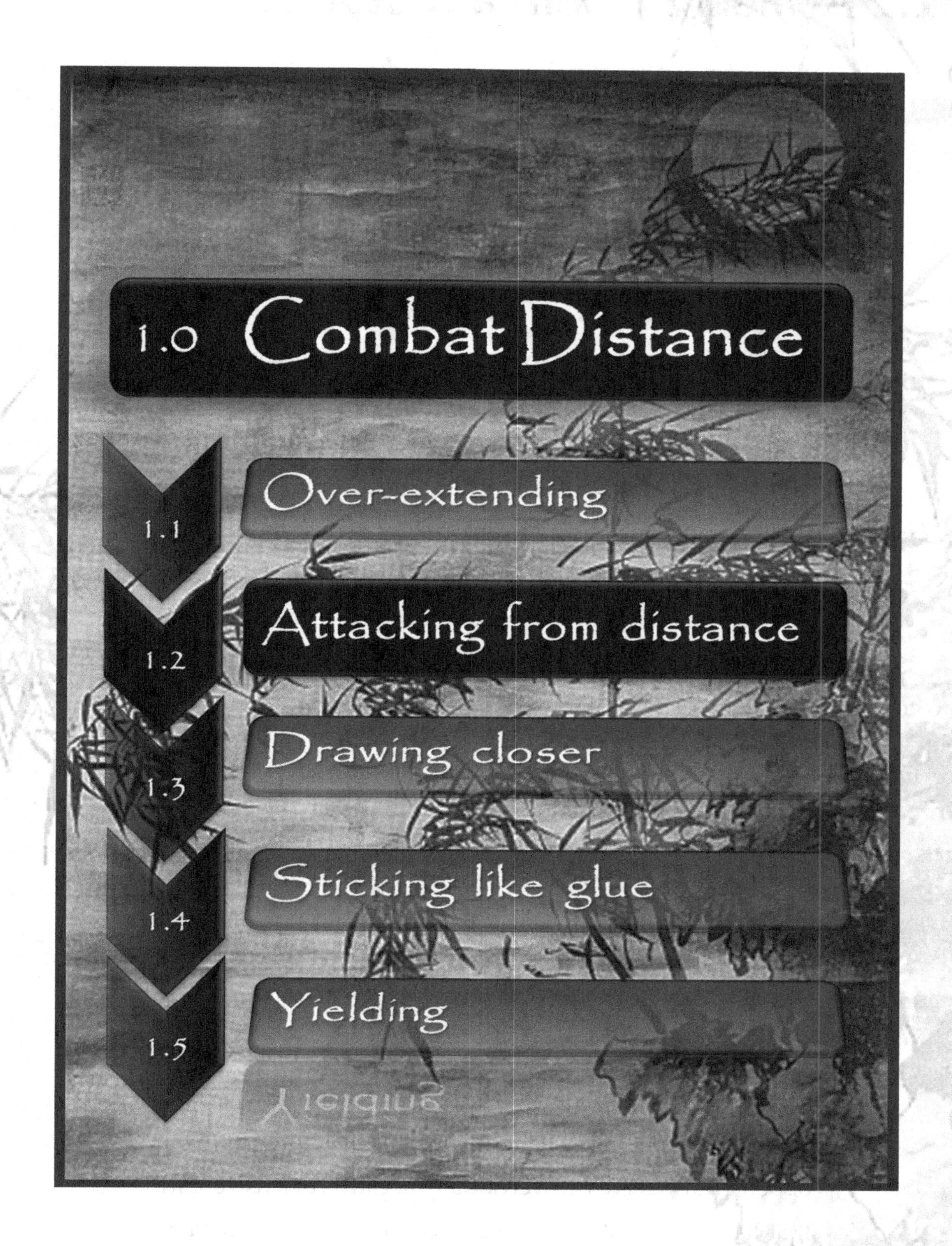
1.0 Combat Distance
1.1
Over-extending
1.2
Attacking from distance
1.3
Drawing closer
1.4
Sticking like glue
1.5
Yielding

1.2 Attacking from a Distance

As outlined in the previous chapter, the *optimal combat distance* is where your opponent must take one step forward to execute any technique against you. The specific distance strategy described within this chapter requires that you immediately fill the void created by a much greater than optimal combat distance between you and your opponent by first utilising a quick half step followed by an immediate large step in order for you to close the distance.

If you experiment by taking a large step first followed by a small step or take two equal steps in order to close the distance, you will quickly realise that taking a small step first gives you a much better physical advantage and increases the power and velocity at which you can successfully execute a devastating technique.

Your physiology and mental attitude are closely related. The same applies to your opponent. This strategy, therefore, also has an added psychological advantage if you take the initiative at just the right moment, forcing your opponent into a defensive posture *(both mentally and physically)*.

This strategy to immediately close such a large distance with such a positive attitude at just the right moment when you perceive an opening in either the posture or attitude of your opponent also serves to override any negative, defensive spirit that has the potential to creep into your psyche by holding back or when you feel overwhelmed. It can also serve to instil a negative, defensive attitude in your opponent, thereby enabling you to exploit any gaps created by your opponent's resulting defensive physiology.

Your opponent may also mistakenly assume that the large space between him or her and you is an opportune time for the person to rest, to regroup, to adjust something, or simply to take a deep breath because he or she mistakenly assume that they will have ample time to mount an effective defence given the distance you have to cover to get to the opponent. This is a serious mistake because in the midst of battle there is no place of safety. You must always be prepared to defend or take the initiative until the threat has been completely neutralized.

Although you might attempt this strategy when facing a much larger opponent than yourself, or someone with a much longer reach than you, please note that this strategy is not the unintelligent suicide launch of a fly into a spider's web! It is also not a desperate or carefree do-or-die move. Attempt it with this attitude, and you may well find yourself skewered by your opponent's weapon! This is not a strategy for beginners.

The course of instruction offered to you within the online *MyeDōjō* training sessions will further walk you through, step by step, a series of practical exercises and drills that will help you to master the above combat distance strategy, which you can then readily apply to your chosen martial-art form.

"Free of weakness ignore the sharp attacks of your enemies: step in and act!"

—*Morihei Ueshiba*

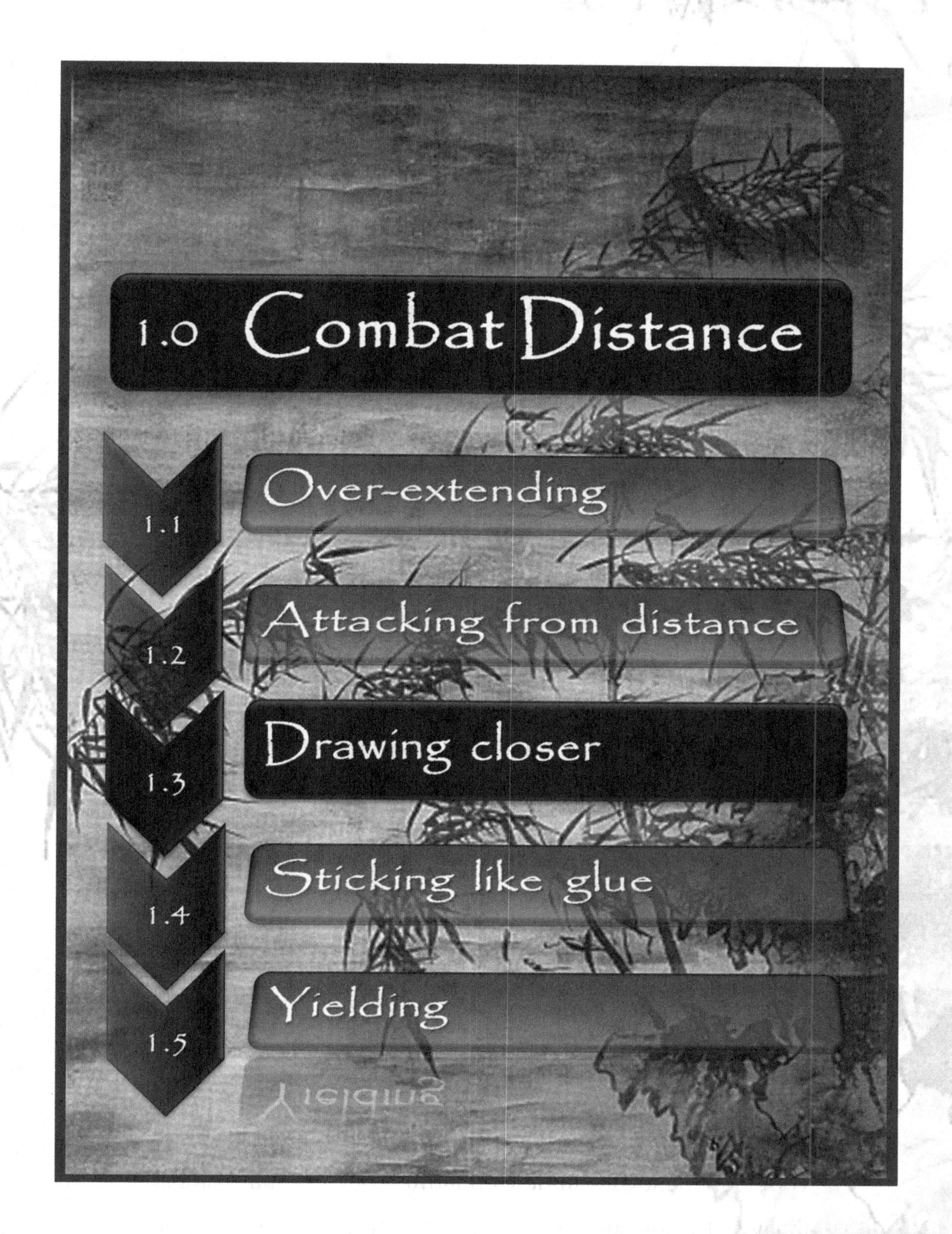
1.0 Combat Distance
1.1
Over-extending
1.2
Attacking from distance
1.3
Drawing closer
1.4
Sticking like glue
1.5
Yielding

1.3 Drawing Closer

As outlined in the previous chapters, the *optimal combat distance* is where your opponent must take one step forward to execute any technique against you. The specific distance strategy described in this chapter involves your ability to subtly launch a strike at your opponent from *slightly closer than* what you consider to be *your* optimal combat distance *(i.e., position yourself slightly closer than where you need to take one step forward in order to make contact with your opponent)*. You will require excellent rhythm, movement, and timing in order not to make this obvious, and not to get hit yourself, especially if your opponent has a reach advantage over you.

In order to pull this strategy off you need to carefully manoeuvre yourself to a distance *only* one or so centimetres closer than what you consider to be *your* optimum combat distance without being hit yourself *(i.e., you have manoeuvred within the radius where it is necessary for you to take one step forward in order to make contact with your opponent)*.

The next part of this strategy is to start to subtly "pull" your strikes or kicks so that they just fall short of making contact with your opponent (*even though you are within your optimal combat distance and don't need to step forward to make contact because you are actually slightly closer to your opponent than the minimum correct combat distance)*. Your intent is to lure your opponent into underestimating your optimal combat distance by not fully extending your strikes without making it look obvious that you are actually pulling your punches or kicks. Once they have taken the bait and closed the distance to where they think they are safe, you start to fully extend your strikes or kicks, which are now actually being delivered from within the minimum radius that defines optimal combat distance *(i.e., you don't now need to take a step forward in order to connect with your opponent).* To your opponent's surprise, all those previous strikes and kicks that they were previously so cleverly dodging by a few centimetres are now finding their mark with devastating effect. They are now unable to react in time because of your stealthy manoeuvring to within the radius where it is necessary for you to take one step forward in order to make contact with your opponent.

There are many creative ways you can experiment with to create this slight combat distance reduction yet present the illusion of an optimal combat distance to your opponent. One simple way is, while both of you are manoeuvring into optimum combat position, when you adjust your position relative to your opponent you move your feet to a position that places you one or so centimetres inside your opponent's optimum combat distance while subtly leaning your torso back so that you appear to be at your opponent's optimum combat distance. When you are ready to launch your attack you simply adjust your torso forward slightly into balance and take advantage of the opponent's now slightly closer combat (less than optimal) distance. But remember, if the gap you create is too close, then your opponent will be motivated to either launch his or her own attack or disengage quick enough to regain balance and then start to attack you from his or her correct combat distance.

Use your imagination. Experiment with and improvise many new ways to create this ever-so-slight reduction in distance so that you can take advantage of your ploy to make your opponent underestimate *your* correct combat distance. The options to create as well as take advantage of this opportunity are only limited by your imagination and ingenuity. This strategy works equally well for striking, grappling, and weapons-based arts. The trick is to remain calm, to keep it subtle, and to not be too obvious or try too hard to trick your opponent closer. Over time, you will recognise many new ways to creatively take advantage of the opportunities presented by this subtle combat distance strategy.

Another thing that you could experiment with is to take a half step forward in response to your opponent's full step forward when he or she attempts to strike you from his or her optimal combat distance. In order for you to make this work you need to strike the opponent on your half-step entry as the strike from his or her full-step entry slips past you.

The course of instruction offered to you within the online *MyeDōjō* training sessions will further walk you through, step by step, a series of practical exercises and drills that will help you to master the above combat distance strategy, which you can then readily apply to your chosen martial-art form.

"The purpose of training is to tighten up the slack, toughen the body, and polish the spirit."

—*Morihei Ueshiba*

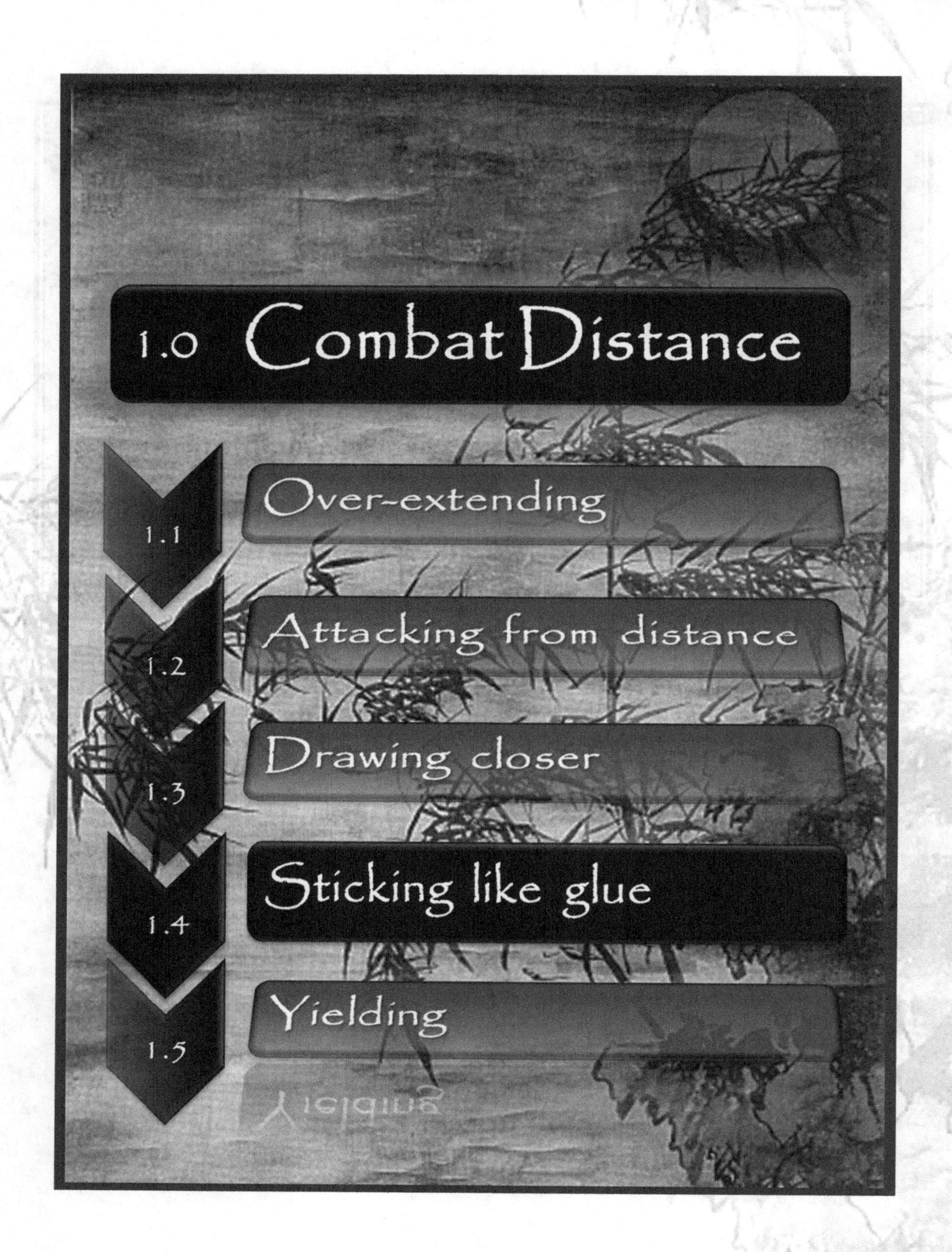
1.0 Combat Distance
1.1
Over-extending
1.2
Attacking from distance
1.3
Drawing closer
1.4
Sticking like glue
1.5
Yielding

1.4 Sticking like Glue

This specific distance strategy requires that you operate within the minimum effective range of any strike and deny your opponent any room to manoeuvre. The idea is to control his or her posture and movement in order to gain advantage. This strategy works equally well with empty hand as well as in situations where there is a disparity in weapon length or striking range, or for empty-hand defence against weapons.

Senior *jujitsu* practitioners understand this strategy very well, and have no problem with close body contact. This is not a strategy to employ if you are timid, or if you are a quiet, shy, or reserved person who needs lots of personal space in order to retain a feeling of calm! To effectively execute this strategy you must have no feeling of withdrawing before you launch a grappling technique or a strike. This is the case whether or not weapons are involved in the altercation. The effectiveness of this strategy is magnified if your opponent is uncomfortable with such close/intimidating offensive techniques and attempts to disengage or step back to create space—leaving him or her vulnerable to attack.

The fundamental prerequisite in order to make this strategy work is to maintain perfect balance, posture, and awareness of your opponent at all times. If any one of these critical elements is lacking, then you will not be in a position to take advantage of your opponent's openings.

There obviously are times when it would be inappropriate to employ this strategy, such as when your opponent has a shorter weapon than you or the strategy would put you at a disadvantage in some way *(i.e., facing multiple opponents empty handed or attempting to grapple in an unsafe environment, where you could be injured on the ground).*

Literally thousands of possibilities exist in the application of this strategy. In order to be proficient you must study them in depth and be prepared to experiment and use your imagination. Be patient and take the time to investigate the application of this strategy fully because it will take much practice! Above all, train with a joyful spirit and a nurturing, respectful attitude towards all your training partners.

The course of instruction offered to you within the online *MyeDōjō* training sessions will further walk you through, step by step, a series of practical exercises and drills that will help you to master the above combat distance strategy, which you can then readily apply to your chosen martial-art form.

"When an opponent comes forward, move in and greet him; if he wants to pull back, send him on his way."

—Morihei Ueshiba

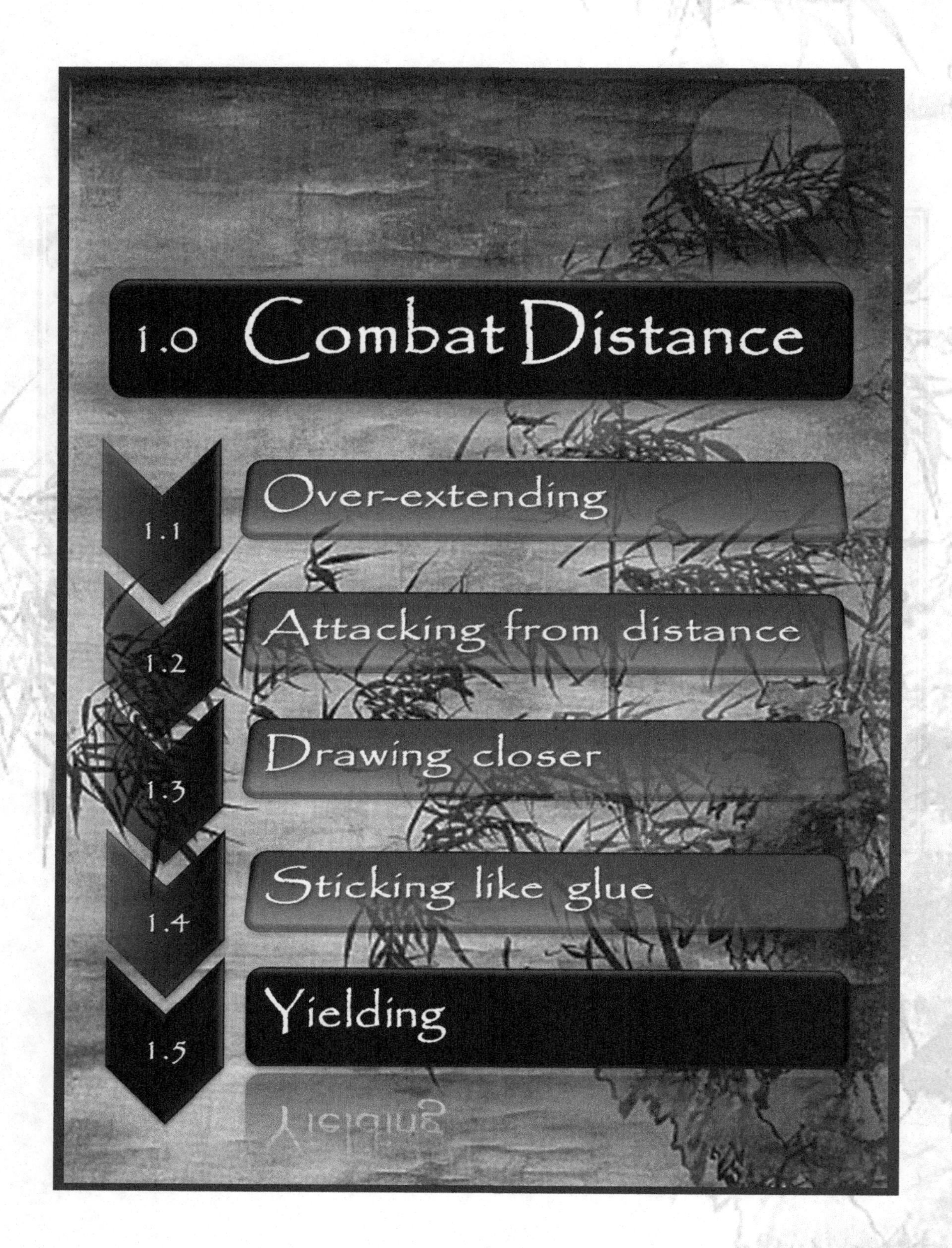
1.0 Combat Distance
1.1
Over-extending
1.2
Attacking from distance
1.3
Drawing closer
1.4
Sticking like glue
1.5
Yielding

1.5 Yielding

This specific distance strategy requires that when you are fighting at reasonably close quarters or grappling, you train out of your body and mind/psyche all desire to attempt to physically force a technique through to completion in a futile manner when the point *(in terms of optimum leverage, timing, or rhythm)* is well past where the technique can be applied with both maximum efficiency and effect. As soon as you hit *any* resistance or there is the *slightest* opportunity for your opponent to counter you, instead of trying to force your originally intended outcome, stay flexible and immediately flow to a new position or technique while remaining totally connected to your opponent. This continuous, unbroken link with your opponent must encompass both your physiological and psychic bond with them.

"Depending on the circumstance, you should be: hard as a diamond, flexible as a willow, smooth-flowing like water, or as empty as space."

—Morihei Ueshiba

The underlying fundamental requirement of all strategy is that there must be a dynamic engagement between you and your opponent on all three levels: the physical, the mental, and the spiritual. When pulled don't resist—*enter.* When pushed don't push back—*open and turn.* If your opponent attempts to deflect your arm or your weapon do not disconnect or offer him or her any feedback in the form of tenseness or resistance—

simply maintain the subtle connection as a reference point while slipping into another position or technique that captures his or her balance or in some way restricts the opponent's effectiveness. This flexibility will allow you to take maximum advantage of the wilful attempt to try to physically force a technique on you.

The same principle holds true if your weapon, empty-hand technique, or any part of your body is immobilised by your opponent. The moment this occurs you must train yourself to immediately let go of the need to force the outcome in your favour by relying on physical strength alone and seamlessly flow, manoeuvre whatever you can, or counter in a way that maximizes your next technique's efficiency and effect.

In order to develop the instinctive skills to effectively implement this strategy you will need to practise a wide range of close-quarters grappling techniques diligently over many years with as many training partners as possible in as many different positions and situations as your experience and imagination allow. In addition, the correct execution of multiple/combination attacks and seamless transitions between striking, throwing, and grappling techniques are a prerequisite for effective application of this strategy. This is equally applicable to empty-hand as well as to weapons interactions.

The course of instruction offered to you within the online *MyeDōjō* training sessions will further walk you through, step by step, a series of practical exercises and drills that will help you to master the above combat distance strategy, which you can then readily apply to your chosen martial-art form.

"Your Spirit is the true shield."

—Morihei Ueshiba

Combat Strategies
1.0
Combat Distance
2.0
Combat Timing
3.0
Combat Momentum
4.0
Control of Centre
5.0
Pre-empting
6.0
Pre-combat

2.0 Combat Timing
2.1
Discerning Rythm
2.2
Varying Speed
2.3
Offence & Defence
2.4
Breath-Cycle Timing

2.0 Combat Timing Strategy

Combat timing is one of the most important things that you must consider and is something that you must learn how to constantly take advantage of in your study of the science of combat strategy. Careful study of your opponent's rhythm will enable you to time your attacks with devastating effectiveness.

The study of rhythm and timing is a very broad and complex undertaking requiring you to be able to adapt and adjust both your rhythm and timing as required to any combination of opponents and weapons being faced. As always, a strong connection with your opponent(s) must be established. As with any communication, once strong rapport is established, you can then lead the interaction at will or take advantage of your insight to control and direct the direction and duration of the interaction.

From the tides to the seasons to your own body's biorhythms, everything and everyone in the universe is in the midst of some rhythmic cycle. An understanding of this rhythm is, therefore, very beneficial, whether you are planning a trip to the moon or simply trying to win a fight. A deeper study of the secret science of combat timing, although outside the scope of this book, delves into the topic of vibration frequency, natural rhythms, and the energy that reverberates from all inanimate objects and animate life forms throughout the cosmos.

With practice you will be able to dictate the rhythm and tempo of the fight: to either speed up the pace or slow it down at will. *The objective is to never allow your opponent to operate at his or her preferred speed.* Conversely, you must train yourself to be able to fight at any speed as the situation dictates. This will require study, imagination, and experimentation in order for you to understand and fully master the dynamic of speed and power as it relates to the topic of combat timing. It is a very fascinating, never-ending, continual process of learning and discovery.

The course of instruction offered to you within the online *MyeDōjō* training sessions will further walk you through, step by step, a series of practical exercises and drills that will help you to master the following combat timing strategies, which you can then readily apply to your chosen martial-art form.

"When an opponent comes forward, move in and greet him; if he wants to pull back, send him on his way."

—Morihei Ueshiba

2.0 Combat Timing
2.1
Discerning Rythm
2.2
Varying Speed
2.3
Offence & Defence
2.4
Breath-Cycle Timing

2.1 Discerning Rhythm

This specific timing strategy requires that you first and foremost train yourself to be able to quickly discern the natural rhythm of your opponent. Your initial objective is to understand the three phases of his or her attack or defence—the start, the middle, and the end phases. You are trying to gain insight into these three phases of any combination of attack or defence techniques being employed by the opponent as well as gauge his or her reaction and the timing of his or her defensive movements to any feints you throw. In order for you to be able to enter between your opponent's attack and defence rhythm, you must first synchronise/match your movement with his or her tempo until you know his or her "beat." You will then have gathered enough intelligence so that you are well prepared to enter in on the half-count between his or her "beat" and deliver a decisive strike or technique.

"At the instant a warrior confronts a foe, all things come into focus."

—Morihei Ueshiba

The critical skill that you need to develop is to take your focus totally off yourself and develop complete empathy/rapport/harmony with your opponent's rhythm and timing. Once this is established your objective is then to attack or counter the opponent between his or her "beats." Once perfected, you will no longer need to rush your offensive or defensive movements. In fact, to an onlooker your efficient and apparently easy defeat of your opponent will look rather calm and unrushed—like a no-contest has just occurred between a master and someone far less experienced; your opponent will appear to be rushing, while you appear calm and able to execute your techniques at will, seemingly almost without effort.

No matter how fast your opponent moves, or how many times the opponent attempts to change the pace of the fight, your techniques are executed *between* the naturally changing rhythms that he or she exhibits throughout the course of the fight. *The ultimate objective is to never let the opponent operate at his or her preferred speed.* This is equally applicable to empty-hand as well as to any weapons interactions. Once you have synchronised with your opponent's beat, you then simply need to speed up your movement on the half-count in order to slip between the counts that you have established as his or her natural rhythm.

In addition, a fast pace set by your opponent or a sudden burst of speed cannot be sustained by him or her for long. It will also be very difficult for you to attempt to match his or her intense rhythm or pace. So here patience is the key. As the opponent's pace and rhythm slows, a small window of opportunity may exist to effectively employ this strategy and strike him or her with devastating effectiveness on the half-count of the opponent's slowing pace.

The course of instruction offered to you within the online *MyeDōjō* training sessions will further walk you through, step by step, a series of practical exercises and drills that will help you to master the above combat timing strategy, which you can then readily apply to your chosen martial-art form.

"Progress comes to those who train and train,
reliance on secret techniques will get you nowhere."

–Morihei Ueshiba

"Even if it is slightly from the way,
it is no longer the way."

—Morihei Ueshiba

2.0 Combat Timing
2.1
Discerning Rythm
2.2
Varying Speed
2.3
Offence & Defence
2.4
Breath-Cycle Timing

2.2 Varying Speed

This specific timing strategy requires that you never allow your opponent to operate at his or her preferred speed. This strategy equally advocates both slowing down as well as speeding up your techniques in order to unsettle or disrupt your opponent's rhythm. A seamless or sudden acceleration and deceleration of your techniques may cause your opponent to underreact or overreact when attempting to block or counter your attacks. By combining this with altering the method or style of your attack, devastating strikes can be landed on an opponent by combining this strategy with any of the distance strategies discussed in the previous chapters. The result of constantly varying the pressure that you subject your opponent to may be to disrupt his or her rhythm enough to completely disorientate the opponent, or at the very least you will make it very hard for him or her to read your rhythm and adjust.

As with the application of any strategy, when employing this *timing strategy*, it is critical that you also train yourself not to be distracted by the strategy; always control your breathing and be able to deliver effective strikes while either accelerating or decelerating your pace. This critical skill must be studied and practiced until all weakness in your attacks or holes in your defence are systematically removed. This is equally applicable to empty-hand as well as to any weapons interactions.

The course of instruction offered to you within the online *MyeDōjō* training sessions will further walk you through, step by step, a series of practical exercises and drills that will help you to master the above combat timing strategy, which you can then readily apply to your chosen martial-art form.

"Always keep your mind as bright and clear as the vast sky, the great ocean, and the highest peak, empty of all thoughts. Always keep your body filled with light and heat. Fill yourself with the power of wisdom and enlightenment."

–Morihei Ueshiba

"If your opponent strikes with fire, counter with water, becoming completely fluid and free-flowing. Water, by its nature, never collides with or breaks against anything. On the contrary, it swallows up any attack harmlessly."

—Morihei Ueshiba

2.0 Combat Timing
2.1
Discerning Rythm
2.2
Varying Speed
2.3
Offence & Defence
2.4
Breath-Cycle Timing

2.3 Combining Offence and Defence

This *timing strategy* requires a decisive spirit and the ability counterattack in one movement that combines offence and defence. Your objective is to simultaneously attack your opponent while defending against his or her intended attack. No feeling of the sequence—first block, then attack—must enter your psyche. Your counterattack must accomplish both attack and defence instantly. You must have no thought of changing targets midstream. Your initial movement must be decisive enough to either finish the fight or disrupt your opponent enough to set you up for certain victory. No doubt or uncertainty should be allowed to infiltrate either your offensive attitude or the decisive execution of your countermovement. Successful execution of this *timing strategy* requires that you first clear your mind of any distractions, negativity, uncertainty, or hesitation—otherwise you may instinctively try to block your opponent's attack, leaving you vulnerable to any combination or counterattack.

This *timing strategy* will enable you to respond spontaneously with devastating speed and power. Your intent must be totally offensive, with no thought of first blocking your opponent's attack. Your entire focus and power must be directed to your offensive point of contact. Do not mistakenly assume that this is simply beating your opponent to the punch. This timing strategy requires that your opponent's attack also misses its intended target by fractions of a centimetre. This is equally applicable to empty-hand as well as to any weapons interactions, but obviously is more important where weapons are concerned.

Another thing that you could experiment with is to combine this timing strategy with a distance-closing strategy by taking a half-step forward in response to your opponent's full step forward when he or she attempts to strike you from his or her *optimal combat distance*. In order for you to make this work, you need to strike the opponent on your half-step entry as the strike from his or her full-step entry slips past you.

Use your imagination. Experiment with and improvise many new ways to counterattack with perfect timing and total commitment. Emphasis must be on simplicity/efficiency of movement, ingenuity, quickness, and effectiveness of your counterattack.

The course of instruction offered to you within the online *MyeDōjō* training sessions will further walk you through, step by step, a series of practical exercises and drills that will help you to master the above combat timing strategy, which you can then readily apply to your chosen martial art form.

2.0 Combat Timing
2.1
Discerning Rythm
2.2
Varying Speed
2.3
Offence & Defence
2.4
Breath-Cycle Timing

2.4 Breath-Cycle Timing

This *timing strategy* requires that you train yourself to instinctively remain aware of whether your opponent is in the process of inhalation or exhalation during the course of battle. In practice this is a very difficult skill to develop, and you will need to practise diligently over many years with as many training partners as possible, in as many different positions and situations as your experience and imagination allows. In addition, the correct execution of multiple/combination attacks and seamless transitions between striking, throwing, and grappling techniques are a prerequisite for effective application of this strategy. This strategy is also equally applicable to empty-hand as well as to weapons interactions.

Your opponent is able to produce *maximum* power only after full inhalation. His or her power progressively depletes in direct proportion to the amount of oxygen the opponent releases from his or her lungs during the exhalation phase of the breath cycle. A careful study of Olympic weightlifters will convince you of this if you have any doubts.

Let's say that your opponent, caught off guard and under pressure, is trying to defend against a barrage of unrelenting upper-level attacks from you. The opponent will naturally contract, possibly cover up and maybe even slightly collapse his or her posture while retreating. As the opponent steps back in an attempt to regain correct combat distance (*maai*) and regain his or her composure the opponent will unconsciously begin to straighten his or her posture. A small window of opportunity has now presented itself that, if you are aware of, will result in an excellent application of this strategy. As the opponent starts to inhale and expand his or her posture a strike to the midsection or taking him or her to the ground will have maximum effect. You must train your response to be instinctive and, therefore, spontaneous. Your opponent's breath must act like a vacuum, which instantaneously draws you into the void created by his or her inhalation. This small window of opportunity, if taken advantage of with expert rhythm and timing, will magnify the effectiveness of your strikes, and throwing or grappling techniques.

Another practical application of this strategy is when, already at very close quarters with your opponent *(either standing or grappling on the ground)*, there may be a brief moment of stillness after he or she has unsuccessfully attempted to execute a throw or grappling technique against you. With such close contact between yourself and your opponent, your ability to know exactly when *(directly after the intense effort of the unsuccessful technique attempt against you)* he or she will start the inhalation phase of the breath cycle. The opponent may even give up on the execution of that particular technique and attempt to quickly transition to something different. Either way, he or she will unconsciously straighten up and/or inhale. Again a small window of opportunity has now presented itself that, if you are aware of it, will once again result in an excellent application of this timing strategy. As the opponent starts to inhale and expand his or her posture, a throwing or grappling technique executed with precision and timing will have maximum effect.

The general "rule of thumb" is attack the opponent when he or she has a depleted level of oxygen supply in the lungs and is just beginning to enter the inhalation phase of the breath cycle. In order for you to not be susceptible to this strategy yourself, you must train yourself to firstly maintain a calm, natural, unforced rhythmic breath cycle (like a pump) throughout battle. Secondly you must develop the ability to keep your abdomen firm while inhaling as well as be able to execute relatively effective strikes and grappling techniques while inhaling or retreating.

The course of instruction offered to you within the online *MyeDōjō* training sessions will further walk you through, step by step, a series of practical exercises and drills that will help you to master the above combat timing strategy, which you can then readily apply to your chosen martial-art form.

"Now and again, it is necessary to seclude yourself among deep mountains and hidden valleys to restore your link to the source of life. Breathe in and let yourself soar to the ends of the universe; breathe out and bring the cosmos back inside. Next, breathe up all fecundity and vibrancy of the earth. Finally, blend the breath of heaven and the breath of earth with your own, becoming the Breath of Life itself."

—Morihei Ueshiba

Combat Strategies
1.0
Combat Distance
2.0
Combat Timing
3.0
Combat Momentum
4.0
Control of Centre
5.0
Pre-empting
6.0
Pre-combat

3.0 Momentum Strategy
3.1
Positioning
3.2
Entering [Irimi]
3.3
Blending
3.4
Pausing

3.0 Combat Momentum Strategy

A well-balanced opponent in a defensive stance is very difficult to strike or throw. The basis of this strategy is, therefore, to first subtly lure your opponents into motion in such a way that he or she is unable to change directions fast enough to avoid your counterattacks. Your ability to effectively interpret and implement this most complex, subtle, and important strategy is a never-ending source of joy and wonder in your study and refinement of the secret science of combat strategy.

A committed person in motion cannot quickly or easily change directions. This particular strategy's premise is, therefore, underpinned by a thorough understanding of the law of momentum, and by your ability to instigate or initiate a specific movement in your opponent in order to take advantage of the impetus, drive, force, and energy exerted by him or her during the course of the committed attack. The subtle and sophisticated strategies with which you instigate or incite an attack from your opponent in which *you* have predetermined either the direction or the offensive technique to be deployed by your opponent has been one of the most closely guarded secrets by great sages over centuries.

You can have tremendous fun using your imagination and experimenting with this most complex and demanding strategy because its subtle nuances can operate at an almost subconscious level based on physiological and psychological factors, as well as subliminal micromovements that are completely undetectable to the naked eye of the uninitiated novice or observer.

"Always try to be in communion with heaven and earth; then the world will appear in its true light. Self-conceit will vanish, and you can blend with any attack."

—Morihei Ueshiba

Once you have lured your opponent's momentum onto a definite course of action (where it is difficult for them to withdraw from his or her committed intent) your subtle and sophisticated movement off the line-of-attack (on the diagonal, yet seemingly directly through your opponent) will result in a devastating counterattack by you that to the uninitiated eye will seem to have an aura of mystique that often invokes incredulous disbelief.

In a more obvious scenario this strategy is most effective against an opponent who attempts to rush or tackle you head-on. Critical components of the effective execution of this strategy are your stance, the placement of your feet, and maintaining your posture and balance during your movement under pressure—but most importantly, your ability to maintain an almost psychic connection with your opponent in order to manipulate his or her intent and the direction of the opponent's movement *almost as if at will.*

This strategy requires a thorough understanding of the previously discussed strategies of combat distance and timing. Once the pragmatic application of these first two basic strategies are understood, then it is time for you to study the application of Newton's first Law of Motion, in which he states that momentum is dependent on an object's mass and velocity. Consideration of these two vital factors is critical to the study of combat momentum strategy.

Use your imagination. Experiment with and improvise many new ways to study the countless ways in which you can manipulate and take advantage of your opponent's motion. The options to create as well as take advantage of your opponent's momentum are only limited by your imagination and ingenuity. This strategy works equally well for striking, grappling, and weapons-based arts. The trick is to remain calm, to keep it subtle, and to not be too obvious or try too hard to provoke your opponent into movement. Over time, you will recognise many new ways to creatively take advantage of the opportunities presented by this strategy.

The course of instruction offered to you within the online *MyeDōjō* training sessions will further walk you through, step by step, a series of practical exercises and drills that will help you to master the following combat momentum strategies, which you can then readily apply to your chosen martial-art form.

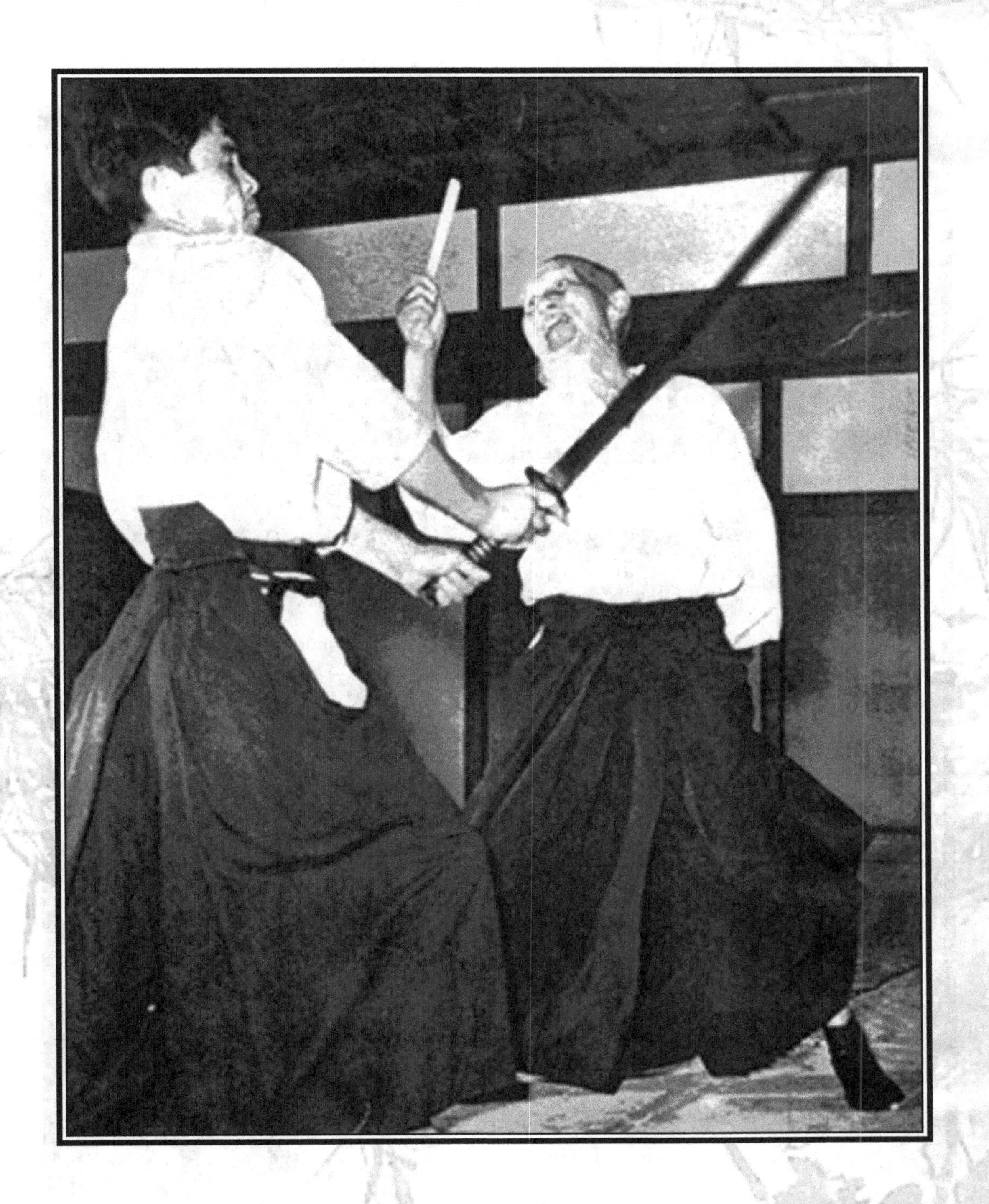

"There exists no measure of time fast or slow. It is not a question of speed. The technique is over before it is begun"

—Morihei Ueshiba

3.0 Momentum Strategy
3.1
Positioning
3.2
Entering [Irimi]
3.3
Blending
3.4
Pausing

3.1 Positioning

This specific momentum strategy requires that you train yourself to move into the most advantageous position while moving off the line of your opponent's attacks. In the execution of this strategy it is critical that the intent of your movement is not to evade and then counter but to move into an optimal position where your countertechnique can be accomplished in one single, continuous motion. This is equally applicable to striking, grappling, and weapons-based arts.

Your training in this combat momentum strategy will take you into the psychological realms, where you can remain unperturbed, not distracted, with a sense of equanimity and poise that will seem surreal to a novice witnessing the skilful execution of this combat strategy. Once you have developed this serene yet highly alert state of mind then—under the pressure of a committed attack—your calm state-of-being will enable you to *respond* with perfect timing instead of reacting in a way that displays suboptimal timing and balance.

Once you have mastered this combat positioning strategy, your deftly accurate movement will merge into the movement of your opponent like light entering a dark room through the slightest crack in the door, instantly placing you in the perfect position to execute an offensive technique most appropriate for that position.

This strategy is best deployed not in reaction to your opponent's movement—*but in response to it*. This implies that you are not surprised by your opponent's movement—but, rather, blend or merge with your opponent's movement based on an initial action or a certain condition that was instigated by *you*, which your opponent reacted to. Your perfect timing, spontaneous movement, and deft positioning would look so simple and natural to a novice observer that he or she might mistake it as a fluke, or say that your opponent got "caught" by a sudden and random move in the heat of battle, which resulted in his or her shocking and devastating loss. The advanced student of combat strategy will know better, and metaphorically *"bow"* to the state of being required to pull off such a feat under the pressure of mortal combat.

Another thing that you could experiment with is to combine this momentum strategy with a distance-closing strategy by taking a half-step forward in response to your opponent's full step forward when he or she attempts to strike you from his or her optimal combat distance. In order for you to make this work, you need to strike the opponent on your half-step entry as the strike from his or her full-step entry slips past you.

Use your imagination. Experiment with and improvise many new ways to study the countless ways in which you can manipulate and take advantage of your opponent's defensive or offensive momentum. The options to create as well as take advantage of your opponent's momentum are only limited by your imagination and ingenuity. This strategy works equally well for striking, grappling, and weapons-based arts. The trick is to remain calm, to keep it subtle, and to not be too obvious or try too hard to provoke your opponent into movement. Over time, you will recognise many new ways to creatively take advantage of the opportunities presented by this strategy.

The course of instruction offered to you within the online *MyeDōjō* training sessions will further walk you through, step by step, a series of practical exercises and drills that will help you to master this combat momentum strategy, which you can then readily apply to your chosen martial-art form.

Left and right, avoid all cuts and parries. Seize your opponents' mind and scatter them all."

—Morihei Ueshiba

3.0 Momentum Strategy
3.1
Positioning
3.2
Entering [Irimi]
3.3
Blending
3.4
Pausing

3.2 Entering [Irimi]

Closely related to the preceding momentum strategy, this specific strategy requires that you train yourself to move directly forward into a very advantageous and dominant position obliquely behind your opponent. Do not confuse the execution of this strategy with simply dodging or sidestepping your opponent's forward thrust. There should be no obvious negative attitude of escape or deliberate avoidance in your forward movement.

You must positively enter into harm's way, as it were, accepting 99.9 percent of your opponent's attack. In order to pull this strategy off effectively you have to deftly slip off the line of your opponent's attack in such a way that his or her offensive commitment is sustained because he or she always thinks that the attack is on target . . . until the last millisecond—when you have already slipped past the opponent and it is too late for him or her to defend. In the execution of this strategy, it is critical that the intent of your movement is not to evade and then counter but to move into an optimal position diagonally to the rear of your opponent—*yet with the appearance of going directly through him or her*—to where your countertechnique can be accomplished in one single, continuous motion. It is as if you are simply filling a void created by a vacuum created by your opponent's forward momentum. This is equally applicable to striking, grappling, and weapons-based arts.

Your training in this secret combat momentum strategy will take you into the psychological realms, where you can remain unperturbed, not distracted, with a sense of equanimity and poise that will seem surreal to a novice witnessing the skilful execution of this combat strategy. Once you have developed this serene yet highly alert state-of-mind, then—under the pressure of a committed attack—your calm state of being will enable you to *respond* with perfect timing instead of reacting in a way that displays suboptimal timing and balance.

Once you have mastered this combat positioning strategy your deftly accurate movement will merge into the movement of your opponent like light entering a dark room through the slightest crack in the door, instantly placing you in the perfect position to execute an offensive technique most appropriate for that position. It is as if you are a cloud of smoke that your opponent has moved forward to strike; however, you have already slipped past him or her—*as if through the opponent.* This strategy is also most effective in order to position yourself outside a circle of multiple attackers.

This strategy is best deployed not in reaction to your opponent's movement—*but in response to it.* This implies that you are not surprised by your opponent's movement—but, rather, blend or merge with your opponent's movement based on an initial action or a certain condition that was instigated by *you,* which your opponent reacted to. Your perfect timing, spontaneous movement, and deft positioning would look so simple and natural to a novice observer that he or she might mistake it as a fluke, and say that your opponent got "caught" by a sudden and random move in the heat of battle, which resulted in his shocking and devastating loss. The advanced student of combat strategy will know better, and metaphorically *"bow"* to the state of being required to pull off such a feat under the pressure of mortal combat.

Use your imagination. Experiment with and improvise many new ways to study the countless ways in which you can manipulate and take advantage of your opponent's defensive or offensive momentum. The options to create, as well as take advantage of, your opponent's momentum are only limited by your imagination and ingenuity. This strategy works equally well for striking, grappling, and weapons-based arts. The trick is to remain calm, to keep it subtle, and to not be too obvious or try too hard to slip past your opponent. Over time, you will recognise many new ways to creatively take advantage of the opportunities presented by this almost magical strategy. This *Irimi* movement appears simple, but the depth of this strategy is most profound, and its unlimited practical application in combat is both elegant and devastatingly effective.

The course of instruction offered to you within the online *MyeDōjō* training sessions will further walk you through, step by step, a series of practical exercises and drills that will help you to master this combat momentum strategy, which you can then readily apply to your chosen martial-art form.

"Opponents confront us continually, but actually there is no opponent there. Enter deeply into an attack and neutralize it as you draw that misdirected force into your own sphere."

–Morihei Ueshiba

3.0 Momentum Strategy
3.1
Positioning
3.2
Entering [Irimi]
3.3
Blending
3.4
Pausing

3.3 Blending

Closely related to the preceding momentum strategies, this specific strategy requires that you train yourself to view the opponent's attacks not as anything dangerous—*but simply as momentum and energy that you can play with*. Instead of clashing with your opponent's energy, you start to explore ways to harness the energy against him or her. This objective attitude of only concerning yourself with totally connecting with your opponent, focusing on directing his or her energy and then unifying your actions with that of your opponent(s) will counteract your natural inbuilt survival/self-preservation predisposition, which can trigger instinctive defensive reactions when attacked. Do not confuse the execution of this strategy with simply dodging, sidestepping your opponent's attack, or stepping straight in for a decisive counterattack. Whether or not you first take an initial step directly forward, the movement of this strategy is either to spiral and blend with the attack or to intercept the attack in the initial stages of the energies-forward momentum. There should be no obvious negative attitude of escape, deliberate avoidance, or wilful offensive mindset in your blending or intercepting movement.

You must positively place yourself in harm's way, as it were, accepting 99.9 percent of your opponent's attack. In order to pull this strategy off effectively you have to deftly and proactively step forward and pivot off the line of your opponent's attack in such a way that his or her offensive commitment is sustained because he or she will always think that the attack is on target . . . until the last millisecond—when you have already blended with the attack or intercepted the energy of the attack in such a way that it is too late for the opponent to defend. In the execution of this strategy it is critical that the intent of your forward, pivoting, or spiralling movement is not to evade and then counter but to meet, merge, and then blend into a position where your countertechnique can be accomplished in one single, continuous motion. Also critical to the correct application of this strategy is that your opponent's posture is disrupted and his or her balance taken—at the first point of contact—between the two of you. Most importantly, there should be absolutely no deliberate attempt by you to "do something" to your opponent—your nonwilful attitude must be one of directing or intercepting the momentum generated by your opponent's aggressive energy. This is equally applicable to striking, grappling, and weapons-based arts.

Your training in this secret combat momentum strategy will take you into the psychological realms, where you can remain unperturbed, not distracted, with a sense of equanimity and poise that will seem surreal to a novice witnessing the skilful execution of this combat strategy. Once you have developed this serene yet highly alert state of mind, then—under the pressure of a committed attack—your calm state of being will enable you to blend with perfect timing instead of reacting in a way that displays suboptimal timing and balance.

Once you have mastered this combat positioning strategy, your deftly accurate movement will merge directly into your opponent—stopping the opponent dead in his or her tracks, or blend into his or her movement like mixing two complementary colours together in a circular motion, instantly placing you in the perfect position to execute an offensive technique most appropriate for that position. The key is to stay connected to your opponent and to move as one, whether you are intercepting the attack or spiralling around it. This strategy is also most effective in order to position yourself outside a circle of multiple attackers.

This strategy is best deployed not in reaction to your opponent's movement—*but in response to it.* This implies that you are not surprised by your opponent's movement—but rather blend or merge with your opponent's movement based on an initial action or a certain condition that was instigated by *you,* which your opponent reacted to. Your perfect timing, spontaneous movement, and deft positioning would look so simple and natural to a novice observer that he or she might mistake it as a fluke, and say that your opponent got "caught" by a sudden and random move in the heat of battle, which resulted in his or her shocking and devastating loss. The advanced student of combat strategy will know better, and metaphorically *"bow"* to the connected state of being required to pull off such a feat under the pressure of mortal combat.

Use your imagination. Experiment with and improvise many new ways to study the countless ways in which you can manipulate and take advantage of your opponent's defensive or offensive momentum. The options to create, as well as to take advantage of, your opponent's momentum are only limited by your imagination and ingenuity. This strategy works equally well for striking, grappling, and weapons-based arts. The trick is to remain calm, to keep it subtle, and to not be too obvious or try too hard to blend with your opponent's movement. Over time, you will recognise many new ways to creatively take advantage of the opportunities presented by this almost magical strategy. Blending movements appears simple, but the depth of this strategy is most profound, and its unlimited practical application in combat is both elegant and devastatingly effective.

The course of instruction offered to you within the online *MyeDōjō* training sessions will further walk you through, step by step, a series of practical exercises and drills that will help you to master this combat momentum strategy, which you can then readily apply to your chosen martial-art form.

3.0 Momentum Strategy
3.1
Positioning
3.2
Entering [Irimi]
3.3
Blending
3.4
Pausing

3.4 Pausing

This specific momentum strategy requires that you create a hesitation and halt, or "pause," the momentum of your opponent just long enough to create a tiny window of opportunity for you to successfully attack. This is accomplished by you apparently dropping your guard in a way that presents a natural, seemingly nondefensive stance and attitude. This has the potential to create a subtle pause of momentum or brief moment of indecision in your opponent while his or her brain quickly tries to figure out whether to attack you. The opportunity may now exist for you to take advantage of this brief moment of mental inertia and instantly launch your attack. This strategy is equally applicable to striking, grappling, and weapons-based arts.

Your training in this combat momentum strategy will take you into the psychological realms, where you can remain unperturbed, not distracted, with a sense of equanimity and poise that will seem surreal to a novice witnessing the skilful execution of this combat strategy. Once you have developed this serene yet highly alert state-of-mind, then—when you seemingly drop your guard—your calm state of being will enable you to *respond* with perfect timing instead of reacting in a way that displays suboptimal timing and balance.

Once you have mastered this combat momentum strategy, your deftly accurate movement will launch an attack at your opponent at precisely the right time during his or her moment of pause/indecision. Alternatively, if your ploy actually lures your opponent to attack, then you can utilise any combination of momentum, distance, and timing strategies to down your opponent.

Use your imagination. Experiment with and improvise countless ways in which you can manipulate and take advantage of your opponent's pause in momentum. The options to create, as well as to take advantage of a pause in your opponent's momentum, are only limited by your imagination and ingenuity. This strategy works equally well for striking, grappling, and weapons-based arts. The trick is to remain calm, to keep it subtle, and to not be too obvious or try too hard to interrupt your opponent's momentum. Over time, you will recognise many new ways to creatively take advantage of the opportunities presented by this strategy.

The course of instruction offered to you within the online *MyeDōjō* training sessions will further walk you through, step by step, a series of practical exercises and drills that will help you to master this combat momentum strategy, which you can then readily apply to your chosen martial-art form.

"Left and right, avoid all cuts and parries. Seize your opponents' mind and scatter them all."

—*Morihei Ueshiba*

Combat Strategies
1.0
Combat Distance
2.0
Combat Timing
3.0
Combat Momentum
4.0
Control of Centre
5.0
Pre-empting
6.0
Pre-combat

4.0 Control of Centre
4.1
Personal Centre
4.2
Opponent's Centre
4.3
Centre to Centre
4.4
Dominate Centre

4.0 Control of Centre

Control of centre is one of the fundamental things that you must consider and is something that you must learn how to constantly become more aware of as well as take advantage of in your study of the science of combat strategy. There are many definitions of *centre*. On a squash court it is the point where the service line intersects the middle line. On a tennis court it is at the centre point of the baseline or even in the middle close to the net if you are volleying. In mixed martial arts (MMA) competition it would be the central area of the octagon. Between two individuals it would be the halfway point between the two combatants. It would be a much more dynamic point where several combatants were involved. Other important things to consider when determining centre would be diverse factors such as the gradient and the terrain where the contest is taking place, etc. On a personal level it could be the centre-line of the body or a very specific central balance point located in the lower abdomen (just below the navel; the Japanese call this point the *hara*). Other important things to consider when determining personal centre would be diverse factors such as whether you are standing, lying down, rolling, etc. In grappling arts much emphasis is placed on the control of your opponent's hips for this very reason—to control balance and, therefore, your opponent's freedom of movement, which serves the dual purpose of not allowing your opponent to execute effective techniques against you while enabling you to execute devastatingly effective techniques against an already off-balance opponent while he or she is incapable of defending himself or herself.

The study of centre is a very broad and complex undertaking requiring you to be able to adapt and adjust your position as required to any combination of opponents and weapons being faced. As always, a strong connection with your centre, your opponent's centre, and your environment's centre must be established. As with any communication, once strong empathy and rapport has been established you can then control and direct the interaction. It is a very fascinating, never-ending, continual process of learning and discovery. Use your imagination. Experiment with and improvise many new ways to study the countless ways in which you can control centre. The options to create as well as to take advantage of and control centre are only limited by your imagination and ingenuity. This strategy works equally well for striking, grappling, and weapons-based arts. The trick is to remain aware of centre at all times. Over time, you will recognise many new ways to creatively take advantage of the opportunities presented by this strategy.

Keep in mind that we are talking about four distinct centres:

1. **Your personal centre**
2. **Your opponent's centre**
3. **Centre to centre**—the dynamic relationship between you and your opponent's centre
4. **Dominate Centre**—a dynamic point within the combat space

The course of instruction offered to you within the online *MyeDōjō* training sessions will further walk you through, step by step, a series of practical exercises and drills that will help you to master the following control of centre strategies, which you can then readily apply to your chosen martial-art form.

The key to good technique is to keep your hands, feet, and hips straight and centered. If you are centered, you can move freely. The physical center is your belly; if your mind is set there as well, you are assured of victory in any endeavour.

—Morihei Ueshiba

4.0 Control of Centre
4.1
Personal Centre
4.2
Opponent's Centre
4.3
Centre to Centre
4.4
Dominate Centre

4.1 Personal Centre

This strategy requires that you train yourself to sustain a calm *inner focus* in your lower abdomen while maintaining alignment of your arms, torso, and hips squarely with an imaginary line running down the middle of your body. In addition, your feeling is one of being *grounded* to the earth while at the same time sustaining your awareness on extending a strong, positive psychological *energy*, which radiates outward in all directions from a specific point in your lower abdomen (referred to in Japan as the *tanden* or *hara*). This aware, alert, and grounded state of mental and physical balance is often referred to as *"being centred" or "maintaining your one point."*

From a practical point of view, you can deliver maximum power from proper balance and connection with the earth, which in turn runs through your hips, torso, and arms. From a psychological point of view, when you diminish thoughts of either self or foe, you free yourself from the tensions and hesitations caused by undue stress and emotion (this state of being is referred to in Japan a *"no mind"* or *Mushin*). In other words, you want to put yourself in the best possible state for combat—both psychologically and physiologically.

An overarching characteristic of being centred is peacefulness. When you are centred you feel peaceful, even in the heat of mortal combat, because you do not allow your psyche and physiology to trigger a stress response of fight or flight. Your mind remains clear and sharp as long as your body maintains a state of centred relaxation (and vice versa).

It might sound weird, especially when talking about mortal combat; however, another important characteristic of being centred is a feeling of *connectedness*. You are radiating, for want of a better word, *love* from every pore of your body, and in turn you feel an overwhelming sense of gratitude, support, and loving protection. Like night and day, *fear and love simply cannot live in the same heart at the same time.*

A third, most practical characteristic of being centred is *confidence*. You feel that you are able to accomplish anything you want, handle any circumstance, resolve any conflict, and figure out a way to win any altercation that may arise. It's a very joyous, creative feeling where anger and frustration are simply nonexistent in light of such a solution-focused attitude.

Last but not least, a most important characteristic of being centred is, again for want of a better word, *harmony*. Closely related to *love* and *connectedness*, you sense a very strong affinity with everything that was, is, and ever will be. All sense of being insignificant, or feeling threatened or alienated, simply does not exist in your consciousness. You are in a place where you are *totally in touch with life.* The practical aspect of this for combat is that the above summarised attitudes/centred state of being will dramatically increase not only your chances for survival, but also instinctively motivate you to derive the best possible outcome for all parties concerned. This is a most significant and important aspect of *Budō.*

The way in which your mind and body communicate with each other lies in the realm of feelings and emotions. Your feelings and emotions are, therefore, a very valuable feedback mechanism. More importantly for combat psychology, the more relaxed and joyous you feel, the more *centred* you are. Therefore, one of the adjunct practices of combat strategy is being able to change your psychological and physiological state *at will.* The significance of this is not to be overlooked or trivialised. You must train yourself to spontaneously and free-flowingly *feel* and *express* gratitude and benevolence until it becomes second nature to you. "What has this to do with fighting?" I hear you ask. Well, *everything.* If you deliberately, consistently, consciously, freely, and willingly give of your resources (time, energy, attention, praise and sincere good wishes, support, and healing, as well as material things, etc.) as if it were an equally significant gift to yourself, others, the environment, and every other living creature, then you will begin to reverse deep-seated patterns of negative thought and behaviour from a scarcity into an abundance mentality. This sense of freedom is one of the important components that facilitate this state of being called *centredness,* and is a clear indication of your progress along the path of *Budō.*

At this point along your path of *Budō,* your connection to your own core—your sense of who you truly are and what you really want—helps establish your connection to the importance and significance of the present moment. Your feelings are interpreted in partnership between your heart and your head. Rationality, reason, and discernment are seamlessly coupled with your instinct and intuition. This further increases your sense of connection and centredness and magnifies all the positive, life-affirming attributes expounded above. This partnership of *heart* and *head* is the point along your path of *Budō* where real magic starts to happen. And it is directly proportional to the level of connection you can establish within yourself. This transformative power of *Budō* results in the elusive joy and happiness that you instinctively yearn for. Once ingrained, your centred connection and courage will inspire others to reconnect to their own centre, heart, joy, intimacy, and power. Your heart then opens up to a new level of *freedom* and *trust* that allows you to fully experience life. This sense of freedom and trust then in turn creates a new level of awareness, which allows you to recognise new opportunities that align your actions with your life-purpose, and naturally draws to it the circumstances and resources required to accomplish your heart's sincere desire. Moreover, the transformative nature of this growing level of *freedom* and *trust* sparks your innate intuitive ability to connect and align with a force greater than yourself. This revelation will anchor a deeper connection with your existence, the universe, and everything in it. This sets the stage for magic to happen on a scale that is currently outside of the realms of your ability to comprehend.

The course of instruction offered to you within the online *MyeDōjō* training sessions will further walk you through, step by step, a series of practical exercises and drills that will help you to master the above combat centring strategy, which you can then readily apply to your chosen martial-art form.

"If your heart is large enough to envelop your adversaries, you can see right through them and avoid their attacks. And once you envelop them, you will be able to guide them along the path dictated to you by heaven and earth."

—Morihei Ueshiba

4.0 Control of Centre
4.1
Personal Centre
4.2
Opponent's Centre
4.3
Centre to Centre
4.4
Dominate Centre

4.2 Your Opponent's Centre

If your opponent is not centred then, by definition, he or she is *off balance*. The transformative nature of your own ability to *centre* and *connect* (refer to preceding chapter) gives you compassionate insight into your opponent's instinctive and compulsive need to attempt to grasp at things and people in a vain attempt to either regain his or her balance, pull others into their negative downward spiral, or simply vent his or her frustration, fear, and anger with aggressive, violent, and destructive patterns of behaviour.

What you focus on tends to expand. So if you maintain your sustained intension on remaining centred and connected while your opponent's primary focus and intent is to dominate or overpower you, then his or her off-balance state will be the opponent's ultimate downfall. This outcome in your favour is assured even before the outset of the confrontation because his or her off-centred focus, intent, and energy will ultimately determine the opponent's fate—*so long as you stay centred and connected.*

A higher state than *selfish* or *selfless* is being *self-full.* I define *self-full* as actions that are a result of mutual benefit for all parties concerned. If you remain *centred* and *connected,* then you will automatically be in a *self-full* state of mind. If your opponent is compelled by fear, anger, or ambition, then his or her impulsive actions will be based in either *fight* or *flight* response. The opponent's motivation will be centred in either selfishness or selflessness. Because they are off balance, they have lost even before they have begun—*so long as you stay centred and connected.*

Your opponent's selfishness is attempting to fill a void in his or her life in inappropriate ways. The opponent's strategic approach to everything is, therefore, seriously flawed. He or she is incapable of considering the situation from a holistic viewpoint. This will severely impact the effectiveness of any strategy he or she attempts to mount against you. Effective and swift resolution of the situation is assured—*so long as you stay centred and connected.*

If your opponent is savvy then he or she will attempt to disrupt your centred state in an attempt to get you to fight off balance—psychologically or physiologically. If your opponent is not centred, then you will sense a gap in his or her concentration, focus, or balance. If the opponent is smart, he or she will also be looking for the same openings in your offensive and defensive movements.

The course of instruction offered to you within the online *MyeDōjō* training sessions will further walk you through, step by step, a series of practical exercises and drills that will help you to master the above centring strategy, which you can then readily apply to your chosen martial-art form.

"Move like a beam of light: fly like lightning, strike like thunder, whirl in circles around a stable center."

–Morihei Ueshiba

4.0 Control of Centre
4.1
Personal Centre
4.2
Opponent's Centre
4.3
Centre to Centre
4.4
Dominate Centre

4.3 Centre to Centre

If you are not centred, then you have little or no chance of truly connecting with your opponent's centre. You will be out of alignment both psychologically and physiologically. The repercussions of this disconnect in combat can be devastating.

The consequences of a habitual lack of awareness and off-centredness can have an equally dramatic impact on your life because you are susceptible to being easily drawn off balance into confrontation and dispute. If you lack awareness, then you will seldom if ever take accountability for the conditions and circumstances you find yourself in because you will always attribute your misfortune, failures, and losses to external forces rather than where the issue more than likely really resides—within yourself and your inability to remained centred and connected.

Once you have mastered the ability to remain centred, your next goal is to instinctively be able to connect your centre to your opponent's centre. This skill will automatically sense any disconnection between you and your opponent. This puts your psyche in a positive, open, and aware state as opposed to a negative, contracted, and defensive state. The ramifications for combat of giving up your personal power and becoming reactive can be devastating. Equally, if not more so, the implications of not being able to connect with the people you interact with on a day-to-day basis in your personal and professional life is obvious. The strategy of being able to maintain awareness of your centre and how to effectively connect with everyone you interact with is common to both effective living and effective combat strategy.

Correct combat strategy requires that you become highly sensitive and acutely aware of any vulnerability caused by either your loss or your opponent's loss of centre, or the instant you feel no connection between you and your opponent's centre. If you are skilled, then the resultant effect of loss of centre on both your or your opponent's psyche and physiology will be immediately apparent. The time you take to reestablish your centre and reconnect with your opponent(s) is critically important because if you do not immediately reestablish your centre and reconnect with your opponent(s) then your progressively contracting spirit and energy may cause you to start to rely on physical strength to control the situation from your off-centred state, which, by this stage, may have escalated to a point well beyond your control.

If your off-centred state becomes habitual, then the compound effect of disappointments and failures on your psyche will result in chronic negative emotional states from which there is slim chance of resurgence. If you are not mindful, you may even start to blame, criticise, and waste a lot of energy trying to physically control every situation and person in your life or, worse still, withdraw from challenges and begin to define yourself based on your failures and disconnections.

I hope that you have gained a small sense of the critical importance of centre not only for combat strategy but also for your life. The course of instruction offered to you within the online *MyeDōjō* training sessions will further walk you through, step by step, a series of practical exercises and drills that will help you to master the above centring strategy, which you can then readily apply to your chosen martial-art form.

"I feel what you call fear,
only I call it 'a call to action.'"

—Morihei Ueshiba

4.0 Control of Centre
4.1
Personal Centre
4.2
Opponent's Centre
4.3
Centre to Centre
4.4
Dominate Centre

4.4 Dominate Centre

In chess, the squares in the centre of the board are considered most important because chess pieces can easily move from the centre of the board to either flank with great speed. A key strategy in squash or tennis is to always move back toward the centre line of the court before playing the next shot because you can quickly access any part of the court to retrieve the opponent's next shot with minimum movement. In the study of combat strategy the same critical importance is placed on understanding the space in which the combat is taking place and your relationship to everything in that space, especially your dynamic relationship to your opponent(s) within that space. Other important things to consider when determining how to dominate centre would be diverse factors such as objects or obstacles in the space, the gradient and the terrain where the contest is taking place, the position of the sun or any glare that may impede vision, proximity to weapons, etc.—the number of variables is endless.

Use your imagination. Experiment with and improvise many new ways to create or take advantage of the space in which the contest is taking place. The options to create, as well as to take advantage of, the many variables related to dominating space are only limited by your imagination and ingenuity. This strategy works equally well for striking, grappling, and weapons-based arts. The trick is to remain calm, to keep it subtle, and to not be too obvious or try too hard to dominate space. Over time, you will recognise many new ways to creatively take advantage of the opportunities presented by this strategy.

The course of instruction offered to you within the online *MyeDōjō* training sessions will further walk you through, step by step, a series of practical exercises and drills that will help you to master the above combat centring strategy, which you can then readily apply to your chosen martial-art form.

"Strength resides where one's ki is concentrated and stable; confusion and maliciousness arise when ki stagnates."

–Morihei Ueshiba

Combat Strategies
1.0
Combat Distance
2.0
Combat Timing
3.0
Combat Momentum
4.0
Control of Centre
5.0
Pre-empting
6.0
Pre-combat

5.0 Pre-empting
5.1
Mushin & Zanshin
5.2
Takemusu Aiki

5.0 Preemptive Combat Strategy

Simply waiting for your opponent to launch an attack is a very risky and dangerous strategy to employ. *Reacting to* instead of *responding with* your opponent is fraught with danger. You must be in motion and "draw out" the opponent's attack, preferably with a movement that severely narrows his or her options in a way that gives you much better odds of preempting or anticipating the opponent's attack or defensive action. The idea is to never allow your opponent to operate to his or her plan. You must force your opponent to move when you want him or her to, on your terms. You must get the opponent to *react* to your movement while you are *responding* to his or hers. This requires you to *act first* and *act decisively* and maintain your initiative by never allowing your opponent to rest or regroup. Obviously this must be backed up with severe training that has conditioned your body to move spontaneously and act instinctively, unimpeded and unhindered by any thought process, deliberation as to the most appropriate technique to employ or, worse yet, impulsiveness, hesitation, or an uncoordinated attempt caused by indecisiveness or by you changing your mind midstream in the heat of battle.

Your training in this combat preemptive strategy will take you into the psychological realms, where you can remain unperturbed, not distracted, with a sense of equanimity and poise that will seem surreal to a novice witnessing the skilful execution of this combat strategy. Once you have developed this serene yet highly alert state of mind, then—when you take the advantage, move first with a decisive spirit, and preempt any movement your opponent offers you—your calm state of being will enable you to respond with perfect timing instead of reacting in a way that displays suboptimal timing and balance.

A prerequisite in order to be able to effectively employ this strategy is for you to have already developed breath control and the ability to not focus on any specific point on your opponent or any weapon he or she might be wielding against you. As with your surroundings, you engage your peripheral vision and observe your opponent as a whole by defocusing your eyes and maintaining your awareness on the big picture without allowing your attention to be drawn into a pinpoint focus on anyone or anything—not even for an instant.

The Japanese term ***mushin*** is defined as *awareness uninhibited by thought*—allowing you to freely respond with action or nonaction as dictated by the particular circumstance without overthinking or analyzing the situation or having any trace of self-doubt. This state of being is a prerequisite requirement for you to be spontaneous and creative.

"Keep your mind as bright and clear as a vast sky—a great ocean and the highest mountain—empty of thoughts."

—Morihei Ueshiba

The Japanese term ***zanshin*** is defined as the sustained focus, heightened awareness, and capacity for creative spontaneous action that resulted from your state of *mushin.*

The Japanese term ***go no sen*** refers to the timing used in a combat engagement where you react to an attacker only after he or she has begun to move.

The Japanese term ***sen no sen*** refers to the timing used in a combat engagement where you react to an attacker at exactly the same moment that he or she has begun to move.

The Japanese term ***sensen no sen*** refers to the timing used in a combat engagement where you initiate the engagement based on a subtle awareness of the opponent's intent to engage you prior to his or her actual attack. This results from a deliberate initiating move on your behalf that prematurely draws out your opponent's intent to attack. The opponent's resulting attack or defense is then seamlessly swept up by your initiative. This is not to be confused with the Japanese term ***"ki musubi,"*** which refers to your ability to precisely match the attacker's movement/intention at its inception, and maintain an unbroken connection with your opponent's movements.

The Japanese term ***yamabiko no michi*** literally means *"the path of the mountain echo."* Deep contemplation of the nature of an echo and how an echo reverberates off the mountains will give you tremendous insight into proper engagement strategy, timing, movement, flow, and the detachment required to effectively employ this most secret and sophisticated preemptive combat strategy.

When you bow deeply to the universe, it bows back; when you call out the name of God, it echoes inside you.

—Morihei Ueshiba

Once you have mastered this preemptive combat strategy your proactive, preemptive movement will simultaneously launch an attack at your opponent at precisely the right moment. Alternatively, if any of your preemptive combat strategies successfully lures your opponent to react, then you can utilise any combination of momentum, distance, and timing strategies to down your opponent.

Use your imagination. Experiment with and improvise countless ways in which you can manipulate and take advantage of your proactive movement towards your opponent. The options to create as well as to take advantage of your positive initiative are only limited by your imagination and ingenuity. This strategy works equally well for striking, grappling, and weapons-based arts. The trick is to remain calm, to keep it subtle, and to not be too obvious or try too hard to take the initiative in order to provoke your opponent into movement and preempt any move he or she might attempt. Over time, you will recognise many new ways to creatively take advantage of the opportunities presented by this most subtle (and one of the most closely guarded secrets of) combat strategy.

Technique-based martial-art systems generally tend to produce rigid, robotic, choreographed partner practice that has little relevance or effectiveness in real-life situations. Real-life situations always involve an infinite number of possibilities that rarely occur the same way twice. The best strategy to adopt in response to any real-life situation is, therefore, the ability to act instinctively from an unlimited variety of techniques and movements. These unlimited techniques and movements will be totally spontaneous and appropriate to the situation at hand because they are in accord with the natural, universal principles of nature. Sophisticated *martial arts* systems, therefore, do not teach set, rigid techniques as such—but a unique set of forms and a mindset that emphasizes the *principles* from which free movement and astoundingly effective martial application are born.

The course of instruction offered to you within the online *MyeDōjō* training sessions will further walk you through, step by step, a series of practical exercises and drills that will help you to master this preemptive combat strategy, which you can then readily apply to your chosen martial-art form.

5.0 Pre-empting
5.1
Mushin & Zanshin
5.2
Takemusu Aiki

5.1 Mushin and Zanshin

Mushin is a Japanese word that is used to describe a special state of being that exhibits an unusually heightened state of awareness—a calm, stable state of mind without fear, anger, anxiety, hatred, or any other negative human emotion that might take you outside the zone of peak human performance. It is a creative state of being without intellectualization that facilitates spontaneous *"right-action."*

A more simple way for you to understand *Mushin* is to recall a time in your life when you felt as if you were in danger, yet remained fully focused, calm, and totally alert. In this state of being your rational mind did not get in the way of your spontaneous, natural, and appropriate actions, which to an observer would have exuded a vitality mixed with calmness, awareness, and a connectedness that was clearly recognizable in your body posture and facial expression. The Japanese also call this state ***"Mushin no shin,"*** or, *"mind of no mind."*

The Japanese term ***zanshin*** can be defined as an alert and aware spirit that resonates from action that emerges from your state of *mushin. Zanshin* is a sustained or heightened state of awareness and mental focus that exists before, during, and after the execution of each of your martial techniques or movements. This *"lingering spirit"* or aware state of mind does not allow even a single pause in your ability to remain spiritually connected to everything and everyone around you. To understand *zanshin* a little better, try to visualize the strong spirit of a master Japanese archer who is in a state of *mushin*. Prior to the release of his arrow he stands transfixed, bow drawn—calm, centred—frozen in a moment in time. Then suddenly, as the arrow tears itself from the archer's fingers, the archer's resonating spirit metaphorically propels the arrow much farther than mere physical strength alone could possibly accomplish. Like riding the waves of an atomic explosion, the arrow is compelled forward from the epicenter of the archer's resonating spirit.

"My students think that I don't lose my centre. I lose my centre as often as you do. I just recognise it sooner and correct faster"

—Morihei Ueshiba

"Fudoshin" is also a Japanese term that is used to describe a state of mind that is not easily thrown off balance and, therefore, appears physically and mentally stable—together with a flexible and free-flowing spirit that is able to receive strong attacks while retaining composed and grounded to the earth—thereby being able to receive energy and yield as appropriate to any situation. It is a very natural state that also facilitates spontaneous *"right action."* In order to be able to conceptualize how your body, breath, and spirit are interrelated and manifest spontaneous *"right action,"* consider how the emotion of happiness and the physical act of smiling are interrelated, and occur simultaneously. Picture how your posture, breath, and resulting actions spontaneously and naturally change when you experience this state of being called *happiness*. Consider also its effect on your spirit. Consider how the physical act of laughing also occurs spontaneously when you get the punchline of a joke. Picture what happens to your physical body—your face, your breath, and your body movements when the laughter erupts from deep within you. In a similar fashion, in a state of *Mushin* there is no discernable gap between intuition and action. This action; spontaneous, natural, and relaxed, will be totally appropriate for the given situation, just as the intensity of your laughter will be directly related to how funny you find the joke.

Budō training enables you to get into this exulted state of being called *Mushin* consistently enough for you to be able to experience its many astounding physical, emotional, and spiritual benefits. The training specifically teaches you how to enter into this creative state of being that contains all possibilities. Like a dynamic stillness that possesses within it the potential for all forms of movement—or like white light having the latent potential to burst into all the many and varied colours of the spectrum, or like the void out of which the *"big bang"* manifested all manner of creation. In that moment of true freedom and empowerment—*where unlimited possibilities exist*—you feel fully alive, centred, and energized. This is the prerequisite state for spontaneous, creative experience.

The Japanese term ***"mizu no kokoro,"*** or *"mind like calm water,"* also attempts to describe this spontaneous, free state of mind as being like a smooth, calm lake that reflects whatever is before it instantaneously, without distortion.

However, in short order after you commence your training, you realize that the harder you *"try"* to achieve this heightened state of being, the further away its attainment seems to get. Your training, therefore, must, by necessity, start with simple yet fundamental skills; such as correct breathing, correct alignment of the body, and where you place your attention. Once understood as something that you cannot force but something that is bestowed upon you—more like a *"state of grace,"* then gratitude will fill your heart as your soul's purpose is allowed full expression. It is from this place that true *martial-art* techniques originate. It is from this place that your personal development will accelerate. It is from this place that your resulting contribution to the world will resonate, and naturally leave a profound and lasting impression.

The Japanese call this quality of the human spirit *"**senshin.**"* It is a spiritual quality that transcends all the other states of mind described above. It is a quality of the human spirit that resonates with the universal quality that protects and harmonizes the universe. Once internalized, a spirit of compassion, contribution, and benevolent service begin to emerge. This becoming more aware of the sacredness of all life means that more of this spirit is being brought into the collective consciousness of all humanity. This then lays the foundation upon which a more enlightened planetary civilization can be built.

5.0 Pre-empting
5.1
Mushin & Zanshin
5.2
Takemusu Aiki

5.2 Takemusu Aiki

Takemusu aiki is a term used by Morihei Ueshiba (founder of *Aikido*) to refer to the highest level of *Aikido*. When you first start training in *martial-arts* you may try to gain some insight into the essence of this unique martial art by researching literature on *Aikido*. You will discover that various translations of the founder's texts define *takemusu aiki* as meaning infinitely generative martial art of aiki. You may find this definition somewhat difficult to understand. The few excerpts that you will find about *takemusu aiki* will also talk about how *Aikido* is not limited to structured, set techniques as taught in class. That once the fundamental principles are internalized it will be possible for you to generate an infinite variety of new techniques as the situation warrants. You may interpret this to mean the instinctive and spontaneous movements of an expert *Aikido* practitioner. You may even liken this skill to operating in the so-called *"zone"* of optimal performance. As you progress in your training, however, this initial interpretation of *takemusu aiki* and its importance to your *specific martial system* will slowly begin to unfold.

During the early phase of your *martial-arts* training, your training partners will cooperate with you in performing specific techniques and drills. Each person will understand his or her role:—who is to attack, exactly what attack to deliver, and the designated defence technique that is to be performed. To ensure safety, these initial attacks will be relatively slow, and the defence predetermined. No resistance will initially be offered by your training partners. Your goal will be to try to imitate the precise manner in which your instructor demonstrated the various techniques. After some training, you may also develop the ability to perform spectacular-looking rolls and high-falls from techniques that are being applied to you. Even though it will all be choreographed, you will feel a certain sense of gratification from your ability to put on such an impressive performance. It will never fail to impress the public, and it will even seem convincing to some people who have had some martial-arts training. Initially, this role-play will be beneficial in order to practice safe falling *(ukemi)* and nurture confidence. At this early point in your training, you may mistakenly think that progress into more realistic martial effectiveness will naturally result from faster and more dynamic execution of these prearranged techniques.

In order to help you to move beyond skillful choreography, once the technical execution of your form is more or less correct, your instructor will direct your training partners to grip you more firmly from a much stronger, static stance and to strike realistically from a more balanced, stable posture. You will, therefore, be confronted with a new challenge. The instant your training partners feel you trying to control them by force, they will instinctively tense up and resist your efforts, or they will continue with a barrage of unexpected attacks that will see your defenses crumble under their onslaught. As a result you may, therefore, start to analyze correct combat distance, timing, and preemptive martial engagement strategies with your training partners to improve your effectiveness. During your more determined efforts, your training partners may even be forced into submission in order to avoid risking ligament injury because at this point in your training you may still be heavily reliant on force and leverage in order to overcome your training partner's strong resistance. The futility of using force against force, however, will be clearly evident to you when the more senior students in the class will easily be able to stop the execution of your techniques or to counter your movements at will. As by this stage you will have been training in *martial-arts* for some time, your inability to realistically defend yourself against multiple attackers who are serious about wanting to take you down might make you question the effectiveness of the techniques in a real-life situation.

In order to help you progress, your instructor will place even more emphasis on your being able to integrate the physical martial-arts techniques with a mental ability to focus your mind on a specific point in your lower abdomen, and extending awareness from that point. Even though you will have been instructed to do this right from the very first day of training, your instructor will now prescribe a much slower, methodical method of training, where execution of each technique is broken down into segments. With your training partners offering such strong commitment, and resisting any attempt to control them, the risk of reverting to your old strength habits will still be high. Therefore, before commencing the technique, as well as during and after the technique, you will be required to stop at specific intervals to make a conscious effort to relax and to reestablish the prescribed mental focus. This slower training will give you enough time to detect any tenseness within yourself, and immediately detect any resistance from your training partners. Several drills and subexercises will then be added to facilitate the feeling of applying effective technique without any force or technical "tricks."

So, instead of seeing your training partner's strong resistance as an obstacle to be overcome, it will now prove to be a valuable feedback mechanism. If you successfully combine the technical elements of the movement with the correct mental focus and nonaggressive attitude, your training partners will be continuously off balance, and will be unable to resist you at any point during the technique. If your focus remains steadfast, and your body remains centred and relaxed, then your training partners will not even be able to regain their balance when you are stationary during the required mental readjustment periods between each segment of the entire technique sequence. At this point in your training, you will begin to analyze and understand how this dynamic control of your training partners has resulted from a direct link between your centre and their centre of gravity through the correct application of each martial-arts technique. When combined with a relaxed disposition that telegraphed no tension, you will be able to capture their balance and maintain control with minimal physical effort.

Once you can accomplish each segment of a technique correctly, you will be instructed to practice the entire technique smoothly, at a pace that does not exceed your ability to remain relaxed and hold your focus steadfast on your centre throughout the entire technique. With practice, your outward appearance will be that of performing a smooth, continuous martial-arts technique. Internally, however, you will be continuously monitoring your ability to remain relaxed, and maintain focus on your lower abdomen, while extending your awareness from a point just below your navel. When the speed at which you attempted to perform the technique exceeds your ability to remain relaxed, or to maintain the required focus and mental extension from your lower abdomen, your old strength habits will immediately kick in.

Your instructor will use analogies, such as a movie reel is just the continuous roll of individual frames, to help you understand that the required mental focus has to be re-created not just segment by segment, but instant by instant before, during and after completion of each technique. Strong *"ki,"* s/he will add, will manifest in the technique with your ability to train your body to remain relaxed, breath correctly, and allow a natural awareness and body-intelligence to emerge out of your stable posture. "From now on," s/he will say, "technique is less important than this ability." "Unlimited technique," s/he will add, "is borne from this ability, so long as you hold to the fundamental principles and employ correct combat strategy."

At this point in your training, *"ki"* will still remain a mysterious, esoteric concept. Confused but resolute, you will continue to train smoothly and slowly as instructed. Your focus will be to stay relaxed under pressure and hold your mental focus on a point in your lower abdomen. With each subsequent training session you will be presented with new challenges that require earnest striving beyond your current mental capability. This will instill within you a humble recognition that the true *"path"* is not so much in achieving victory over your adversaries, but in the ability to persist with earnest, constant striving beyond your current capability towards the attainment of higher physical and mental principles.

At this level, your conscious mind will be required to stay alert in order to gauge whether you are remaining truly relaxed, and whether you can maintain correct posture and mental focus under increasing amounts of pressure. At the same time, however, a prerequisite requirement for success will be that your mind is free from the incessant chatter of a calculating and dominating conscious ego—an ego molded by past experiences, beliefs, and subconscious emotional responses. So, even though you need to engage your conscious awareness in order to train slowly and methodically, the risk that your ego's strong *sense-of-self* will kick in and override your mental focus will remain ever present. The moment this happens during execution of the technique, control over your training partner's centre of balance will vanish, and all that will remain will be your ego, intent on victory, grappling with an increasingly resistant opponent.

In order for you to move beyond ego dominance, you will need to train yourself to be able to consistently and seamlessly maintain the required mental focus *at every instant* throughout each technique. You will be required to allow no thought of contention or fighting to infiltrate your deep, calm, inner concentration. Eventually, the ability to maintain this state of being will take priority over any desired outcome of victory. At times, differentiation between your training partners and yourself, as well as everything else, will seem to dissipate. This dynamic, meditative state will evoke an awe-inspiring glimpse into the greater reality of your connectedness with everything and everyone.

At this point in your training, you will start to gain some insight into why *O'Sensei* described *takemusu aiki* as a mystical experience that filled his heart with joy and gratitude. You will also gain insight into what *O'Sensei* meant by his comments about becoming more open and receptive to the natural laws that dictate unforced and harmonious interaction. At about this time, you will also begin to contemplate why *O'Sensei* described *takemusu aiki* as the linking back to an original, undifferentiated consciousness that he stated was the underlying theme behind all spiritual disciplines.

With the practice of *budō* I believe *O'Sensei* invites you to recognize that we are all an integral part of a connected universe, and not an isolated entity that is separate or apart from it, or from each other. Through profound study of the human spirit, *O'Sensei* understood that the human psyche is fragmented by individual likes and dislikes, by judgment between what is good or bad and between what is right or wrong. *O'Sensei* realized how this sense of separation breeds competition, anxiety, desire, resentment, frustration, and fear in the world, resulting in escalating hostility and confrontation between nations and races. *O'Sensei* also realized that, without an effective self-transformative discipline, such as *Aikido*, these emotions would continue to reinforce the growing sense of

"The heart of Aikido is: true victory is Self-Victory . . . integrate the inner and outer factors of practice . . . If you think about winning you will lose everything . . ."

—Morihei Ueshiba

segregation and isolation that has become so prevalent in our own society today. In the early phase of your *martial-arts* training this sense of personal separation will be clearly reflected in the struggle you exhibit with your training partners.

> ***"Do not get caught up with the form and appearance of a challenge. The Art of Peace has no form—it is a study of the spirit."***
>
> *—Morihei Ueshiba*

Some spiritual teachers preach a doctrine of having to let go of, or destroy, the ego. As your training unfolds, however, you will realize first-hand that ego and authentic personality are equally essential players in your life. Authentic personality is the vehicle for spirit to evolve through form. You may also come to realize that it is incorrect to want the ego to disappear altogether. You will learn how to open your awareness so that your ego and your authentic personality work together in alignment. Your goal is to build an *"emotionally intelligent"* ego. You may also realize that, ironically, only a strong, mature ego has the power to take on the task of empowering your spirit to emerge forthright from behind an immature, overly protective but ultimately isolated and lonely mindset.

> ***"Ultimately, you must forget about technique. The further you progress, the fewer teachings there are. The Great Path is really No Path"***
>
> *—Morihei Ueshiba*

Your own personal experience will teach you that *martial-arts* training has the potential to cultivate your innate ability to interact spontaneously and naturally to the world around you from a deep-seated understanding of your connectedness to nature, as well as to other people. As a result, you may come to appreciate why *O'Sensei's* concept of *takemusu aiki* is so fundamentally important to *martial-arts* practice. It is what differentiates training that is focused on the utilization of sophisticated martial strategies and techniques to gain victory over perceived adversaries, *versus* a physical and mental discipline that's goal is to reestablish a sense of connectedness with your fellow human beings and with the creative life force of nature (*ki*). The way in which you approach your *martial-arts* training will determine whether you move closer to this realization.

"Aikido is not an art to fight or to defeat an enemy . . . The essence of Aikido is to tune oneself with the functioning of the universe, to become one with the universe . . . Martial artists who are not in harmony with the universe are merely executing combat techniques, not Takemusu Aiki"

—Morihei Ueshiba

"If you do not link yourself to True Emptiness, you will never fully comprehend the path of Aiki"

—*Morihei Ueshiba*

Combat Strategies
1.0
Combat Distance
2.0
Combat Timing
3.0
Combat Momentum
4.0
Control of Centre
5.0
Pre-empting
6.0
Pre-combat

6.0 Pre-combat Strategy

6.0 Precombat Strategy

There are many definitions of *winning*. In theory the ideal victory is where the confrontation is won with no physical contest. In order to accomplish this your options may, therefore, range from employing relatively simple/less sophisticated strategies such as appearing either much weaker or much stronger than you really are to the development of a comprehensive mitigation or preemptive strategy that addresses a vast array of potential scenarios that could be categorised as either ethical or nonethical in nature:—the exploration, discussion, and debate of which is outside the scope of this book.

Staying healthy, and developing better athleticism, fitness, strength, stamina, and vitality, encompasses a vast topic that is also outside the scope of this book, and includes hygiene factors, how well you breathe, sleep, eat, and stay hydrated—not to mention stress management, relationship management, and other diverse topics such as financial management skills in order to reduce your day-to-day stress levels. In fact, anything that could adversely impact your physical or mental performance must be considered carefully. The vast topic of combat preparation encompasses many factors that are simply outside the scope of this book, including the research and use of technology, weapons, transport, clothing, supplies, and good interpersonal skills. These are just a few of the many factors that could impact your success or failure. A casual attitude to the many complex and varied factors relating to combat preparation will inevitably place you in a disadvantageous position or circumstance that you may not be able to compensate for in the heat of battle. An awareness of how well you and your opponent are conducting research, gathering intelligence, and managing all the above stated precombat variables are vital skills in your study and practical application of combat strategy.

Physical endurance, mental health, and spiritual resilience are all equally important factors that determine success or failure. Careful study must, therefore, also be given to the many psychological and physiological factors that need to be considered in your precombat strategy that may positively or adversely impact either yourself or your opponent. With study and experience, you will better prepare yourself for victory. The message here is that you should not adopt a casual attitude to combat preparation strategy. By staying alert to the many factors that influence success and defeat you will be in a better position to develop a systematic, disciplined approach to preparing yourself for combat. Over time, you will recognise many new ways to creatively take advantage of the opportunities presented by this strategy.

"It is necessary to develop a strategy that utilizes all the physical conditions and elements that are directly at hand. The best strategy relies upon an unlimited set of responses."

—Morihei Ueshiba

7.0 Competition
7.1
7 Rules of Free-form Drill
7.2
Correct Behaviour
7.3
Offence & Defence

7.0 Competition

Budō is practiced as a pure traditional martial-art form and not as a sport. Full application of technique in a competitive sporting event does not result in death. Full application of technique in a real-life martial contest most certainly can, especially if multiple attackers or weapons are involved. In preparing for competition, the scope of your development is, therefore, limited to a specific set of pragmatic skills that are essential in order to ensure victory over others within the constraints stipulated by the governing body of the particular sport in which you are competing.

> ***"From ancient times, budō has never been considered a sport."***
>
> *—Morihei Ueshiba*

Competition is healthy if undertaken for the right reasons and if bound by rules and regulations in order to ensure safety and fairness to all participants. Competition drives the excellence you demand from yourself and others, but if undertaken for the wrong reasons it has the potential to be detrimental to your long-term happiness—firstly, in terms of lifelong debilitating physical injuries and, secondly, in terms of supporting and perpetuating a mindset that is not necessarily helpful to individual or collective progress.

Some people, although disciplined and skilled, avoid competition because they fear injury, loss, or ridicule. Others have a deep-seated sense of inferiority or, conversely, try to protect a fragile sense of superiority that they subconsciously fear might be shattered if they were put to the test in open competition. Shyness and bravado are just two of the many ways some people try to mask deep-seated feelings of either inferiority or superiority.

The values held by our culture, and your constant comparison of what material or social successes other people have achieved, have the potential to instill in you either a sense of superiority or inferiority. In our materialistic societies, you generally receive approval based on your appearance, your possessions, your intellectual capacity, your social status, and any successes you achieve in business, entertainment, or sport, or even who you associate with. In order to obtain this approval, you may spend a lot of time and effort polishing the outer image that you present to the world. This fragile outer image thinly masks the high emotional effort required to support it. The emotional energy needed to constantly prop up or protect this vulnerable outer image affects everything you do and every relationship you have.

From an early age, you have been categorized as a high, medium, or low performer in academic and sporting endeavors. You were no doubt acutely aware of your designated position relative to every other child in school. Based on this social conditioning, you may feel the need to enter into competition for the wrong reasons. For in that moment of victory, when you thrust your fist into the air, you feel good about yourself and your place in the world. For that moment, the self-doubt that so strongly questioned your own abilities from childhood is drowned out by your victorious battle cry. Each successive victory, in a deep psychological way, not only validates your status as being important and valuable, but also temporarily satisfies a more base need for you to feel that you are worthy of love and approval.

This insatiable desire for success and recognition creates a life filled with intense judgment and comparison of you against others. Regardless of whether the comparison, or competition, goes in your favour or not, your feeling good or bad about yourself is still dependent on whether someone else is either better or worse than you. It is, therefore, necessary for others to fail in order for you to feel good about yourself. So how secure can you really be if you always feel vulnerable to anyone who possesses the potential to beat you? Undertaken for the wrong reasons, competition, therefore, can set you up for a lifetime of comparison, jealousy, envy, disappointment, and disapproval of others, and of yourself. Gripped by these emotions, you may turn petty, negative, and spiteful. Slowly, year upon year, these negative feelings can affect your health and can contour the wrinkles on your face according to the intensity of your emotions.

"There is no enemy . . . You are mistaken if you think that budō means to have opponents and enemies and be strong and fell them. There are neither opponents nor enemies in true budō. True budō is to be one with the universe"

—Morihei Ueshiba

Even consider that any one of the millions of people currently living in third world countries or in underprivileged conditions might easily be able to defeat you if they were fortunate enough to be given the same opportunities and resources that you have been given. The reality is that there will always be someone who is bigger, faster, stronger, better, smarter, or more successful than you are. Even if you are victorious, it probably will only happen if you specifically train to peak at the right time. Either way, your position as *"number one"* in any field of endeavour will only last for a relatively short period of time. Being the best at anything is, therefore, just another illusion created by your fragile ego. It is just another enticement that requires much effort but is not sustainable for long. The truth is that your unique talents and skills are more than enough for you to contribute to the world in significant and profound ways that are much more fulfilling than the temporary elation of victory over any perceived adversary. If there is a contest, it must, therefore, be fought within yourself, because *true victory* implies freedom from the negative aspects that plague your human condition. Your ongoing journey or path then continues to be one of joy and of continuous evolution, wonder, and discovery. Effective martial-art skills are only a useful by-product of such intense study. In the true spirit of *yoga* and *budō,* your training, therefore, becomes one of continuous refinement of body, mind, and spirit—as well as *self-full* service to your training partners. In a world full of conflict and competition, it represents enlightened interaction that benefits everyone you train with—and, therefore, ultimately reflects the potential for this *enlightened interdependent behaviour* to spread throughout all of humanity.

In the practice of *budō*, correct breathing, combined with specific physical and mental conditioning, gradually discards the negative habits of mind that previously limited your potential. You slowly start to develop a solid feeling of self-worth that is underpinned by a clear understanding of universal values and principles. You do not feel so threatened or anxious about winning or losing, or whether you get other people's approval. You begin to use criticism, and life experiences, either positive or negative, to better understand your strengths and weaknesses. You start to become more tolerant of your shortcomings, as well as those of others. You disapprove less. Bit by bit, your need to win over others in order to gain respect gives way to an inner strength that does not deflate when reassurance and approval are not in constant supply. Instead of avoiding risk and expending energy in a futile attempt to control your world and the people within it, you begin to welcome change and the evolution it brings. Over time you let go of your need to feel superior or inferior, together with the accompanying baggage of self-criticism, comparison, judgment, disappointment, jealousy, and envy. As a result, your attitude gradually shifts from individualism to *interdependence*, connecting you as one among many, as opposed to one above, or below, many. This leaves you feeling positive towards yourself and others. As a result, your mind gradually becomes your servant and not your master. Ironically, this state of mind maximizes your chances of gaining the love, happiness, and approval that you so desperately wanted to win in competition.

Budō training calms the mind, enabling you to physiologically centre yourself and expand your awareness beyond the world of winning and losing, us versus them, and friends versus enemies. This enlightened frame of reference broadens your awareness further than what you previously allowed yourself to feel. This heightened awareness also widens your perspective to include the larger social and environmental issues that affect our whole planet. A growing sense of spirituality, where you begin to tune into something bigger than yourself, also awakens a deep concern for the whole planet and all its inhabitants. This conviction, emerging from your growing understanding of yourself, creates within you the courage to act with a certainty that is grounded in your understanding of fundamental universal principles. You remain calm and centred under pressure, and strive to live a life of authenticity that is true to your values.

In your *martial-arts* training, you therefore seek victory not over others, but over yourself. *Overcoming is not the same as transcending.* In order to transcend your past conditioning you need all the emotional maturity that you can muster. To inappropriately dissipate all your physical and emotional energy in competitive pursuits in order to satisfy a constant need for emotional gratification is counterproductive to your ultimate purpose in life. Competitive sport is designed to produce a winner. In real life, we all need one another to succeed.

Unless you compete for a living, the attitude of needing to constantly prove that you are superior is a clear display of your lack of understanding. In a professional sporting contest such as boxing or mixed martial arts (MMA) you are required to *"leave it all in the ring,"* but in real combat you need to conserve every ounce of your energy that you have in order to have something in reserve to be able to escape if wounded, to help others, or to regroup for further battle that has no referees and no time limit.

Once you *truly* realise that effective and sustainable results only manifest from the superior state of being relaxed (as opposed to a chronically stress-induced state caused by constant tension and struggle), then the proverbial *"light bulb"* of this wisdom will illuminate your understanding. This transition from *struggle to relaxation* marks a major milestone in your development. Based on this understanding, the resultant enlightened behaviour you exhibit with your fellow training partners will be obvious. This attitude cannot be faked—not for long anyway—*and definitely not under pressure.* Unless you strive for this ultimate ideal, then you, your training, and your ability to support your training partners will forever dwell in the realm of mediocrity because of your inflexible approach. This noble path is not always easy. However, the path, the training, and the lifelong relationships formed are always immensely rewarding.

A *martial-arts dōjō* is, therefore, a place where you come to build relationships based on trust—*trust in yourself and trust in your training partners.* A place where you *nurture* and give your *full attention* (i.e., *love*) to yourself, your environment, and everyone you interact with. Ego and contest have no place here. Yes, in the real world, violence does exist, but you can only hope to prepare yourself with the skills that do not contribute to its escalation. If we fail in this task—*as humanity*—then we all fail—game over! The real challenge is, therefore, not to try to change the world, but to simply change you—*from the inside out.* Then all ignorance, arrogance, resentment, struggle, fear, and delusion will simply drop from you. They will all fall from your body as easily as a scab falls from a flesh wound because it has fulfilled its usefulness. If this is not your purpose—if this is not a fundamental goal of your training—then you should not waste your time in this pursuit. You would only increase the likelihood of injuring yourself and others. No fruit would come from all your competitive endeavors—except for maybe the acquisition of a few trophies that you would then have to dust for the rest of your life.

A good friend of mine once said to me, ***"I do not want to leave my mark in clay and sand. I want to leave it where it will last forever:—in the hearts and minds of my fellow human beings."*** If you too can embrace this ideal, then you will automatically be graced with the patience, discipline, and fortitude required to embrace this path that we call *budō.* My friend's message was to not leave your life to chance or circumstance, but to live your life *on purpose.*

In *yoga, dharma* means *"living your unique purpose."* But how do you find meaning and fulfillment in ways that are congruent with who you really are in order to best serve and contribute to the world? Life will not only ask you to answer this very important question, but it will demand that you also do something very courageous; it will expect you to chart your own path, based on your uniqueness, and contribute to others, not for reward or recognition, *but as a gift*—a gift that is equally and simultaneously given to yourself as well as to everyone else. Anything short of this self-full service will result in a very joyless existence.

Ultimately, then, the art of victory over adversaries—*the art of war*—must become the art of effective relationships and interdependence—*the art of peace.*

This cycle of *war* and *peace* naturally oscillates on our planet. On a much wider scale, within a universe that must contain every opposite in order to maintain equilibrium; within this delicate balance; within this ever-present, ongoing interplay of the naturally opposing forces of war and peace; lies the path of *Budō* and the path of *Yoga.*

7.0 Competition
7.1
7 Rules of Free-form Drill
7.2
Correct Behaviour
7.3
Offence & Defence

7.1 Seven Rules of Free-Form Drill

The following chapter describes the seven key rules or guidelines relating to free-form sparring against single or multiple attackers.

1. Strict Instructor Supervision

Under no circumstances can sparring of any kind be performed except under the strict and direct supervision of a qualified instructor. It is the instructor's responsibility to ensure that all health and safety principles and formal Code of Conduct and Health and Safety guidelines are strictly adhered to at all times.

2. No False Ego

Remember, these drills only attempt to simulate real-life physical confrontation. It is not real fighting. Real fighting is over much faster—with potentially serious physical (not to mention legal and physiological) ramifications for all parties concerned. There are many more considerations in real-life situations that require specific strategic and tactical knowledge, skills, and action outside the scope of this sparring drill. All *martial art* drills and sub-exercises should be performed quite unemotionally, in a detached manner, without any desire to succeed or any apprehension of failing. Your objective is to study and learn from your mistakes in a safe and nurturing environment.

3. Respectful Attitude

Please approach these drills with the correct attitude and respect for all concerned because these dynamic drills are designed to enhance the confidence, skill level, and spontaneous creativity of both the attackers as well as the defender. Everyone is learning to let go of fear and their fight/flight response in order to perceive more attack-and-defence opportunities and to be able to appropriately act in spontaneous, innovative, and creative ways—and improvise, depending on the situation.

4. Etiquette

As there is no choreography or predetermined outcome, either party in the engagement can be "victorious"; however, victory is not the aim of the drill. Gaining skills in the pursuit of knowledge based on correct principles is the chief aim of the sparring drill. Specific etiquette is, therefore, observed as follows: before and after each drill, all participants formally bow to each other to signify their sincere attempt to see how they perform under pressure and to highlight whether correct principles are understood. The sincere pursuit of knowledge and mutual gain places respect before ego or the desire for victory.

5. Focus on Skill Development

The focus should be on correct breathing, centring, perfecting combat strategy, and the development of spontaneous creativity and improvisation within the constraints of the drill.

6. Healthy Contact

The drill is performed without any protective gear. Contact is "healthy" if given and received appropriately. The idea is to get the body used to contact, whether it be strikes, kicks, or grappling.

7. There Are No Rules

Within this context, all creative forms of defence and offence are permissible, with no rules apart from the mandatory safety behaviour for free-form sparring outlined overleaf, and those pertaining to the prescribed drill speed based on the skill level of the participants.

7.0 Competition
7.1
7 Rules of Free-form Drill
7.2
Correct Behaviour
7.3
Offence & Defence

7.2 Behaviour for Free-Form Drill

The following points describe the appropriate behaviour relating to free-form sparring against single or multiple attackers. The objective is to simulate the pressure of reality in order to facilitate spontaneity and creativity in a safe and nurturing environment.

- No choreography or premature falling. No deliberate over extension or off-balance attacks. Do not execute a soft attack and then just wait to be countered. No deliberate missing (i.e., healthy contact)! When striking, kicking, or grappling, make sincere, proper contact—without inflicting pain, while strictly observing all safety requirements of the drill.

- Both attackers and defender must maintain the same predefined drill speed. Absolutely no sudden accelerated movements that exceed the instructor's predefined drill speed.

- Attackers remain aware and put increasing pressure on the defender based on instructions from the instructor. Do not stop until clear instruction is received from the instructor or an injury is accidentally sustained that requires immediate treatment.

- Be innovative and use your imagination. The use of weapons and/or creative utilization of any available surrounding object that might come to hand are all permissible. Any object in the room, or anything at all if the exercise is performed outdoors (e.g., trees, stones, water, etc.), can be utilized creatively—while strictly observing all safety requirements of the drill.

- All attackers must acknowledge when they have received a legitimate strike or submission hold—*tap out*—and then disengage to a safe distance before attempting to reengage. If the defender is taken to the ground, the attackers are to continue to strike or grapple—safely—until the defender taps out.

"There are no contests in Aikido. A true warrior is invincible because he or she contests with nothing. Defeat means to defeat the mind of contention that we harbour within."

—*Morihei Ueshiba*

7.0 Competition
7 Rules of Free-form Drill
7.1
Correct Behaviour
7.2
Instructor Guidelines
7.3

7.3 Free-Form Drill Instructor Notes

The following chapter describes instructor's notes to ensure that ***appropriate behaviour*** is maintained relating to free-form sparring against single or multiple attackers. The objective is to simulate the pressure of reality in order to facilitate spontaneity and creativity in a safe and nurturing environment.

- Drill speed is performed at an appropriate level based on the skill level of all participants in order to ensure the development of correct physical, mental, and technical skills. Drill speed must always start slowly and be increased in speed and intensity during the course of the drill based on the skill level of the participants.

- Immediately correct anyone that consciously or subconsciously increases the speed of his or her attack or defence above the prescribed drill speed. This is especially the case when vital points of the body are targeted or any weapon is introduced.

- Only simulated attacks—strictly *no contact* to the following body parts: eyes, ears, groin, breasts, or neck. Also, strictly only simulation of close quarters yelling into ears. If attacks are successfully simulated in an appropriate manner, the receiving participant must tap out and disengage to a safe distance before being permitted to reengage.

"The techniques of the Way of Peace change constantly. Today's techniques will be different tomorrow."

—*Morihei Ueshiba*

8.0 The Way of Budō
8.1
What is Aikido?
8.2
What is Yoga?
8.3
What is Aikido-Yoga?

8.0 The Way of *Budō*

The Japanese word *Budō* is derived from the words *"bu,"* meaning *martial* or *combat,* and *"dō,"* meaning *way* or *path.* The word *"dō"* originally comes from the Chinese word *"Tao" or "Dao,"* which originated from the philosopher *Lao-Tsu* and means *way* or *path* to understanding the underlying natural order of the universe. *Budō* is, therefore, the great tradition of martial arts as a way to self-actualization.

Bu-jitsu focuses on martial methods for combat effectiveness, whereas *bu-dō* focuses on martial ways for spiritual development. Training based on the great tradition of *budō,* therefore, emphasizes a deeper level of awareness of both mind and body. With this awareness comes a connectedness that expands your consciousness beyond your isolated, solitary concept of yourself as separate from the rest of nature. Take, for example, the natural process of breathing, and how it ties you to the rhythm of nature and the many forms of plant life that produce oxygen, and represents one of the thousands of symbiotic relationships that you rely on every day for your survival.

In its most basic and functional definition, the Japanese word *dō-jō* is used to denote a training hall. Its literal translation, however, is *"place of the Way."* From ancient times, a *dōjō* was the name given to a building devoted to the practice of *Zen,* a place where people came to strengthen and refine mind, body, and spirit in pursuit of enlightenment.

Zen is a distillation of mystic Buddhism, which originally migrated from India through China and then, finally, into Japan. It depicts a philosophical way of life that is typically Japanese but retains the mysticism of India, the Taoists' deep appreciation of nature, and the practicality of Confucianism.

The *Kegon School* in Japan adopted Buddhism around 1200 AD. They named their version of Buddhism Zen. As in Buddhism, the various schools of *Zen* attach great importance to sitting meditation *(zazen). Zen* also inherited the Buddhist belief in the perfection of our original nature, with enlightenment resulting from a realization of this fact. The experience of enlightenment in *Zen* is called *satori.*

Zen has had an enormous influence on all aspects of the traditional Japanese way of life. Its influence extends to the arts of painting, calligraphy, gardening, the tea ceremony, flower arranging, and various martial arts such as archery, swordsmanship, and *aiki-do.* Each of these disciplines is known in Japan as a *"dō"* or *"way"* toward enlightenment because each utilizes *Zen* to train the mind to be calm, present, and spontaneous. All of these disciplines require you to perfect technique; however, mastery is only realized when technique has been transcended, and your spontaneous actions are no longer inhibited by any debilitation or intellectual processes such as evaluating and judging.

Like Zen, *budō* trains your mind and body to be calm and tension-free, and firmly grounded in the present moment. Through awareness practices, you learn how to go beyond thinking—into a state that can only be described as meditation in motion, while remaining relaxed and totally aware under pressure—fully alive in the joy of the moment.

The objectives of *Budō, Dō* and *Zen* are complementary. *Zen* seeks self-perfection through passive means, such as meditation. *Dō* seeks self-perfection and personal transformation through active means, such as the practice of *budō*. At the highest levels, *budō* becomes a kind of moving meditation (*do-zen*), in contrast to the sitting meditation of *Zen* (*za-zen*).

In *budō* your nonviolent movements are, therefore, in direct response to your attacker's aggressive intent and actions. In this expanded state of awareness, you are merely dealing with the dynamic interaction and interplay of energy that exists in time and space. You are, therefore, not actually involved in the conflict; however, you are capable of effortlessly controlling any aggressors by absorbing their movements into your *"eye of the storm"*—where your calm mind, fully present in the moment, can act and respond appropriately.

The respect with which you approach your training partners, therefore, lies in the fact that you recognize the intrinsic value and significance they add to your life. This openness and trust lays the foundation upon which true learning flourishes. The freshness, newness, and spontaneity that come from this kind of approach also acknowledge the need to continually challenge your old paradigms and explore new ways of being. You, therefore, approach your training partners as if they were the most important people in your life at that moment in time.

Each and every training session begins and ends with this attitude of respect and acknowledgement of everyone's quest to move beyond the physical—into the spiritual, sacred realms of his or her being.

Before you can let go of your limitations, you first have to notice them; otherwise, you will remain ignorant of their effect on everything you do, and every relationship you have. *Once aware*, it is then possible for you to start the process of letting go. Therefore, while training, you are encouraged to remain constantly attentive to the workings of your own mind, and how it affects your physical movements and balance. It gives you an opportunity to look again—*more carefully*—at how your mind works. As you slowly become more aware of how many limitations you actually have, you begin to appreciate the negative impact that an untrained mind has on the quality of your life. This process of going within yourself, of becoming more aware, raises fundamental questions about what is truly important in your life. A growing awareness of your own true nature emerges—along with the growing conviction to act in accordance with your values.

Emphasis on only the physical or martial aspects of *budō* alone, therefore, creates a serious misalignment with its true, intended purpose, which is *yoga (self-transformation).* Misalignment with this purpose can lead to incomplete, harmful, and even destructive training methods. Moreover, this misalignment has the potential to increase the mounting residue of desire, greed, anger, obsession, and envy that builds up in your heart as a result of incorrect living. Practicing forcefully is also counterproductive to moving deeper into the subtle layers of your being because it adds new layers of subconscious habits based on incorrect conditioned responses, which only result in more delusion and suffering, and ever increasing identification with your body. In *yoga,* increased identification with anything that is impermanent, such as the body, is called ignorance (*avidya*). So, with respect to your *Budō* training, ultimately, *what* you practice is not as important as *how* you practice (and, therefore, also from *whom* you receive instruction).

8.0 The Way of Budō
8.1
What is Aikido?
8.2
What is Yoga?
8.3
What is Aikido-Yoga?

8.1 What is *Aikido?*

Aikido is an astonishingly efficient and effective martial art. The founder of ***Aikido***, Morihei Ueshiba (1883-1969), was one of the greatest martial artists in modern history. *Aikido* training integrates several martial systems, including empty hand (*tai-jutsu*), wooden sword (*aiki-ken*), wooden staff (*aiki-jo*) and knife (*tanto*). Instead of clashing with an attacker's physical strength, the self-defence techniques of *Aikido* blend with your attacker's movements using the dynamic engagement strategies and spherical motion evolved from the devastatingly effective techniques of *Japanese swordsmanship*—enabling you to effectively defend yourself against multiple armed or unarmed attackers without the need to employ the destructive punching and kicking techniques that characterise other combat arts.

8.0 The Way of Budō
8.1
What is Aikido?
8.2
What is Yoga?
8.3
What is Aikido-Yoga?

8.2 What is *Yoga?*

Yoga is the science of effective self-mastery, personal transformation, and self-realisation.

Developed in India over a period of some five thousand years, yoga has branched into the various forms known today by names such as *Râja-Yoga* (Royal Yoga), *Hatha-Yoga* (Power Yoga), *Karma-Yoga* (Yoga of Action), *Jnâna-Yoga* (Yoga of Wisdom), *Bhakti-Yoga* (Yoga of Devotion), *Mantra-Yoga* (Yoga of Power-Sounds), *Tantra-Yoga* (Tantric Yoga), *Kundalinî-Yoga* (Yoga of the Serpent-Power), and *Laya-Yoga* (Yoga of Absorption). Many other physical and spiritual disciplines and practices exist, and are continually developing as humanity evolves.

All around the world, *yoga* has proven itself to be a very practical and effective way of facilitating physical and mental well-being, developing core stability, enhancing co-ordination, and activating your personal power through enhanced focus, awareness, and proven breathing and meditation techniques. The word *yoga,* however, actually stems from the Sanskrit term *"yuj,"* which means *"to unite"* or to *"yoke"* with a *Higher Truth.* This *"union"* is the realization of your intimate connection with all of creation. This ultimate reality or *Truth* is free from all dogmatic and artificial belief systems because it is derived from personal experience. As implied by the addition of the word *"Yoga"* to the word *"Aikido,"* the ultimate purpose of *"Aikido-Yoga"* is self-transformation and self-actualization.

"Some people are only interested in the devastatingly effective self-defence aspects of Aikido—but beyond that Aikido-Yoga offers amazing possibilities for personal growth."

—*Jules Aib*

The yogic process is sometimes referred to as a path to enlightenment, but it's more helpful to look at it as a simple recognition of *what* and *who* you already are. You just need to slow down enough to realize that all the answers lie dormant within yourself—so it is counterproductive for you to attempt to find the answers to the great mysteries of life from someone else because that can only be accomplished by going within yourself—*with awareness.* Modern-day teachers, utilizing a vast array of physical and spiritual disciplines evolved by humanity over millennia, can certainly give you a great start, but in the end it all comes down to you. To give up accountability to any one person or discipline is to abdicate responsibility for your own personal growth. Employing this flawed strategy is foolish. Common sense tells you that you must first build a strong, flexible, and healthy body. In order to accomplish this, you must work on ways to allow your nervous system, respiratory system, digestive system, glandular system, skeletal structure, and the thousands of other interdependent systems within your body to work in harmony. Then, utilizing proven yogic methods developed by humanity over millennia, you can safely move into the practice of sensory deprivation, and then into the sublime power of focused concentration and meditation, where the profound answers of life await you.

"Yoga helps me to discover where
I am struggling, striving and forcing.
Then it is a matter of letting go."

—*Jules Aib*

8.0 The Way of Budō
8.1
What is Aikido?
8.2
What is Yoga?
8.3
What is Aikido-Yoga?

8.3 What is *Aikido-Yoga?*

Aikido-Yoga is the art of effective self-defence, self-discovery, and self-mastery. The art seamlessly integrates the traditional training methods employed by the Japanese martial art of *Aikido* with the ancient science of *Yoga*. Far more than a separate study of *Aikido* and *Yoga* in isolation from each other, the teaching methods of *Aikido-Yoga* provide a seamless integration of the two disciplines.

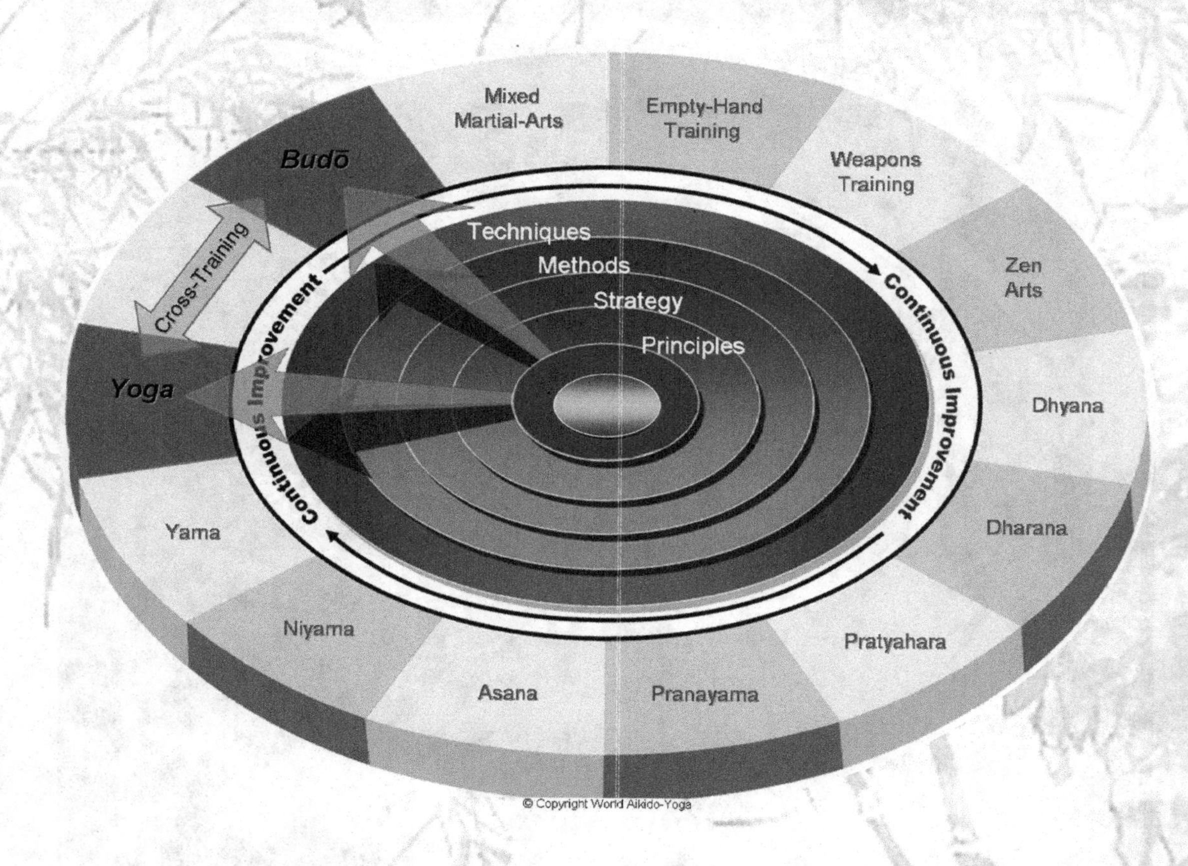

The specific yoga training incorporated into *Aikido-Yoga* includes *yama* (restraints), *niyama* (observances), *asana* (yoga postures), *prânayama* (breath control), *pratyahara* (withdrawal of the senses), *dharana* (concentration), and *dhyana* (meditation).

Aikido-Yoga, therefore, taps into ancient yogic knowledge and practice that has been honed into a science in the East over millennia.

Aikido-Yoga training, therefore, not only establishes a direct connection back to the great traditions and disciplines offered by both *yoga* and *budō* but, more importantly, offers you a pragmatic method of authentic self-discovery that is at the forefront of a new generation of enlightened growth.

Although this system called *Aikido-Yoga* is unique and distinctly different to other *Aikido* styles, we do not claim that it is the only, or even the best form of *Aikido,* or *Yoga,* for that matter. That would be absurd. It is, however, one of the authentic representations of *Aikido,* and is a genuine form of *Yoga* practice which is still alive today. Being alive, it is, by definition, vibrant and evolving and, therefore, relevant and appropriate for today. It accomplishes this by not living in the past or focusing on perceived or desired future results. *It simply allows you to live effectively in the present moment.* This may sound rather simplistic at first, but consider how the most direct, simple approaches are often the most effective. You may realize that the simple act of harmonizing your life with its ultimate purpose, and finding a balance between *being* and *doing,* can be very powerful because that helps you let go of the past, walk the middle path, and arrive at the truth, which is secreted in the present moment.

Aikido-Yoga's holistic approach to personal transformation, therefore, integrates the physical, emotional, mental, and spiritual elements of your self-development. It also works to retain more of your body's life force (*prâna, chi* or *ki*) through yogic breathing and mental discipline. Gradually but surely, the breathing, meditation, and other self-transformation exercises of *Aikido-Yoga* facilitate an awakening of your mind to the more subtle, spiritual aspects of your being. It is an extremely valuable, thoroughly enjoyable, immensely satisfying, and a very rewarding activity worthy of serious pursuit.

The training methods of *Aikido-Yoga*, therefore, not only give you a direct link back to the great tradition of *budō* that has evolved from the humble beginnings of human conflict but, more importantly, provides you with a proven set of yogic principles and practices that empower you to follow your own path of authentic self-discovery.

9.0 Hard & Soft Styles
9.1
The Hard Styles
9.2
The Soft Styles
9.3
Merging Hard & Soft
9.4
Beyond Hard & Soft

9.0 Hard and Soft Styles

Budō encompasses many profound martial arts. Its depth and breadth are infinite. It, therefore, lends itself to an infinite variety of interpretations, approaches, and applications based on the varied personality types, backgrounds, experience, and maturity of those who sincerely attempt to delve deeply into its fathomless mysteries and secrets. For this reason, there is a multiplicity of *martial-arts* styles prevalent throughout the world today. These styles can be loosely categorized as being either *"hard"* or *"soft"* in their approach and application.

> ***"The techniques of the Way of Peace change constantly. Today's techniques will be different tomorrow. Do not get caught up with the form and appearance of a challenge. The Art of Peace has no form—it is the study of the spirit."***
>
> *—Morihei Ueshiba*

9.0 Hard & Soft Styles
9.1
The Hard Styles
9.2
The Soft Styles
9.3
Merging Hard & Soft
9.4
Beyond Hard & Soft

9.1 The Hard Styles of Aikido

Morihei Ueshiba, the founder of *Aikido,* had exposure to many different empty-hand and weapons-based martial arts. He was also very heavily influenced by Sokaku Takeda, who taught him *Daitō-ryū Aiki-jūjutsu*. The so-called "hard-style" Aikido schools trace their lineage back to the more severe combat-oriented style of *Aikido* practiced and taught by the founder pre-World War II, when, some say, he was at the height of his physical strength and combat effectiveness. Some of these early direct students of the founder combined their knowledge of other martial disciplines, in which they were already highly skilled, with whatever exposure they may have had to the founder in these formative years, when he was just beginning to develop the spiritual principles and more subtle application of technique that formed the basis of modern *Aikido*. Their individualized versions of "hard" style *Aikido* were then actively promoted and spread throughout the world.

These so-called *"hard"* styles of *Aikido* prefer to focus on the combative aspects of this very effective martial-art form. Their emphasis is on martial effectiveness. Some, therefore, hold competitions, while others endeavor to simulate realistic combat situations designed to be effective in real-life situations or to be competitive against other combat arts. Their approach is based on a sincere desire to practice an effective combat art, and in doing so, derive the many other benefits associated with such dedicated, earnest *bu-jutsu* training.

"Fiddling with this and that technique is of no avail. Simply act decisively without reserve!"

—*Morihei Ueshiba*

9.0 Hard & Soft Styles
9.1
The Hard Styles
9.2
The Soft Styles
9.3
Merging Hard & Soft
9.4
Beyond Hard & Soft

9.2 The Soft Styles of *Aikido*

Morihei Ueshiba, the founder of *Aikido,* was very heavily influenced by mystical Shintoism, and in particular by a certain Shinto sect called *"Omoto-kyo."* Morihei became captivated by the charismatic leader of this sect—Deguchi Onisaburo (1871-1948)—and delved deeply into its many esoteric religious rituals and spiritual practices. The *"soft"* style schools are strongly influenced by the spiritual and ethical ideals of the founder. Their approach is, therefore, based on a strong appreciation of the founder's spiritual teachings, and upon the underlying moral and ethical principles that they strongly associate with their practice.

Therefore, at the other end of the spectrum from the *"hard"* styles, these so-called *"soft"* style schools of *Aikido* trace their lineage back to the more physically forgiving, more flowing style of *Aikido* that was demonstrated by an aging Morihei Ueshiba post-World War II, when, some say, his techniques were endowed with superhuman energy *(ki)* after years of focusing on his spiritual development.

"True Budō calls for bringing the inner energy of the universe in order, protecting the peace of the world as well as preserving everything in nature in its right form."

—Morihei Ueshiba

9.0 Hard & Soft Styles
9.1
The Hard Styles
9.2
The Soft Styles
9.3
Merging Hard & Soft
9.4
Beyond Hard & Soft

9.3 Merging Hard and Soft

Although the sincere practice of *bu-jitsu (martial methods, for combat effectiveness)* penetrates deeply into the heart of *bu-dō (martial ways, for spiritual development)*, there is a clear distinction between the two.

Aikido's traditional martial-arts lineage can be traced back to the devastatingly effective martial-art forms that evolved out of ***Japanese swordsmanship.*** Based on the realities of centuries of real-life, no-holds-barred, close-quarters martial encounters, the Japanese Samurai's martial combat strategy was naturally honed devoid of any of the artificial rules and regulations that characterise modern martial-arts tournaments. Based on this lineage, *Aikido* is, therefore, an exceptionally effective method of martial arts training that is true to traditional *bu-jutsu* ideals. From a martial perspective, the strategic defensive and offensive movements of ***Japanese swordsmanship*** upon which *Aikido's* movements and combat strategy are based always place you in a position where a decisive outcome can be determined in the blink of an eye.

The saying *"one cut, one kill"* is used to point to this principle of one lightning quick, decisive action during a martial encounter involving swords. From a spiritual as well as a practical perspective, in the fraction of a second that it takes for two swords to flash past each other, in order to survive, you must be fully in the present moment—calm, alert, fully awake, and aware. In that moment of truth, you must also cut yourself off from any fear. Therefore, in order for you to be truly present, consideration of past and future (the playground of the ego) must cease to exist for you. Because your extraneous thoughts must cease to order for you to be effective in combat, there exists the potential for you to move beyond your thinking, calculating mind just long enough for you to be able to catch a glimpse of the ever-present moment that you live in. Wisdom comes from the insight that links the experience of this moment of truth to each and every moment of your life, and thereby facilitates your awareness of one aspect of spiritual growth espoused in all *bu-dō* and *Zen* arts.

The term *"the external now"* defines each moment as being both the culmination of all of eternity, as well as its brand-new beginning. The present moment is inextricably interlinked with all of the past and all of the future. In fact, each moment is simultaneously the death of the old and the birth of the new. Each moment contains within it either the possibility of the creation of something completely new, or alternatively, it contains the energy to sustain its intention to re-create or reproduce that which already exists within the dynamic, infinite continuum of slipping from the past into the future. Because trying to put this concept into words is so difficult, if not impossible, it is not uncommon for the modern-day quantum physicist to sound very much like a yogi when trying to describe how he or she interprets reality.

Ultimate *Reality* or *Truth* is not understood by *"doing."* It is experienced by simply *"being."* It is the art and the dance of all of existence—to simply be. The art of simply *"being"* is the ultimate goal of every human *"being."* It is from here that life is empowered with infinite possibilities. It is, therefore, from here that life can be lived to its full potential. And it is from this fathomless source that *budō* draws its power.

So, instead of philosophizing, intellectualizing, or discussing that which cannot be described, *budō* simply goes straight to the heart of the matter, and trains you to experience reality for yourself. Your training, therefore, teaches you not only how to *"sustain your intention,"* but how to *"re-create it"—moment by moment, instant by instant*—until your consciousness, metaphorically speaking, seamlessly merges into the ongoing continuum of reality. It is from here that your spontaneity and creativity is born.

"The circle symbolizes serenity and perfection, the source of unlimited techniques."

—Morihei Ueshiba

9.0 Hard & Soft Styles
9.1
The Hard Styles
9.2
The Soft Styles
9.3
Merging Hard & Soft
9.4
Beyond Hard & Soft

9.4 Beyond Hard and Soft

The word "martial" in the English language relates to war, but the word *"Yoga"* in India *(as does the word "do" in Japan)*, relates to a journey of personal development and transformation leading to self-realisation. In the final analysis, *budō* is, therefore, essentially human potential development training.

> ***"The best strategy relies upon an unlimited set of responses"***
>
> *—Morihei Ueshiba*

However, this training also helps us face the reality of violence from the perspective of an integrated human being. *A wholly integrated person cannot easily be controlled or manipulated by greed, intimidation, or fear.* In general, however, when push comes to shove, most people automatically experience a fight or flight response. The issue, therefore, is whether you are able to move beyond your automatic response mechanisms and focus your attention on *"what is the desired outcome?"* and *"what is the most appropriate course of action in order to achieve that outcome?"* Yes, if you must fight, you fight, but your fighting will possess the quality of compassion, and of caring. You will not react like a wild animal. You will fight with wisdom, with intelligence. In fact, in most situations, conflict can be settled before it comes to violence. Even in the rare times when actually engaging an adversary is necessary, direct physical confrontation may not be the wisest course of action. The training of your character is, therefore, all important.

In *budō* you equally cultivate strength and flexibility of both body and character. Some people, however, simply want to learn the technical skills of combat. If you only train in this way you will be stuck in technique, and will severely limit your ability to progress into the more subtle, spiritual dimensions of the art. The development of character must, therefore, go hand in hand with development of technique. What good is your life if you are the best fighter in the world, but have not cultivated any worthwhile relationships, or made any worthwhile contribution to society? Yes, people may fear you, but can they trust you? How will you be remembered by your family and your friends, and by society? At the inevitable end of your mortal existence, *"What will you have accomplished?" "What legacy will you have left behind?" "What will you have learnt?"* And, *"Who did you love?"* Above all, these will be your most important questions.

"Emphasis on the physical aspects alone is futile, for the power of the body is always limited."

—Morihei Ueshiba

Life is a very precious gift. One aspect of self-defence training is, therefore, to maintain and preserve life. But, the fact is, nobody gets out of this world alive. At some point in time the inevitable will happen—you will die. But in the meantime, while alive, everything you do directly impacts everyone you interrelate with, and indirectly impacts the destiny of our planet.

Therefore, it is vitally important for you to discover what your true purpose is. Once understood, instead of continually fighting with others, your attitude, the approach you take, and all of your actions will automatically align towards that purpose.

10.0 Advanced Practices
10.1
Prana - Chi - Ki
10.2
Mind & Body Connection

10.0 Advanced Practices

In the practice of *martial arts*, an initial challenge is to develop skills that move both the *"nage" (person receiving the attack and executing an appropriate self-defence response)* and the *"uke" (person offering the attack and receiving the technique)* beyond cooperative choreography—into the realm of enlightened interaction. However, while either *uke* or *nage* are beginning to learn the moves appropriate to their respective roles, a natural degree of cooperation and nurturing must exist, and must be clearly understood by both of them. Training fast without appropriate skills is very dangerous for both the *uke* and the *nage*, especially where weapons training is concerned. Once this is clearly understood, and the *nage* has a reasonable grasp of how to perform the technique, the *uke* is instructed to apply increasing amounts of strength and purposeful intent when attempting to grapple or strike the *nage (note: but initially only at a speed and intent that nurtures growth and ensures the safety of both)*. This offers both parties better feedback on the futility of trying to clash force against force, tussle with resistance, pit physical strength against strength, or willfully try to force an outcome in their favour. Valuable knowledge and information is, therefore, gained by both parties.

As each person increases his or her level of skill in this role-play, a growing trust engenders a willingness to move on to higher levels of training—with a complete sense of safety. The requirement at the next, yet still basic, level of training is to make the martial technique work while being performed at a slow, methodical, mindful, measured pace—against strong resistance or realistic strikes *(performed up to but not surpassing the skill level of either training partner).* Throughout the exercise, the *nage* sets his or her mind on sustaining an unbroken, continuous stream of conscious intention (which can be referred to as activating or animating one's "*ki,*" or "vital life-force energy"). When the *nage's* continuous, sustained intent is in harmony with everything around him or her—even the attackers—we call that *AI-KI* ("*AI*" meaning to harmonize with "*KI*"—the omnipresent life force of creation). Even if the technique is broken into segments—and performed very slowly—the strong connection between the *nage's* stable centre of gravity and the attacker's unstable centre of gravity is clearly evident—even when the *nage* stops between each segment of the technique in order to study correct form or recalibrate the required mental focus.

After a strong grounding in correct technical form, speed, timing, and martial engagement strategy is introduced into the training to further develop the student's ability to remain relaxed, breathe under pressure, and attempt to maintain the correct mental focus. At this level of training, both the *uke* and the *nage* demonstrate their ability to control themselves and cooperate under pressure. However, once the basic form of a technique has been learnt by the *nage,* and the *uke* is able to safely fall/roll/protect himself or herself from injury, the *uke* is instructed not to just passively stand there and simply allow the *nage* to perform the technique on him/her, but to be alive and sensitive to what is happening—with an acute awareness of the connection points that are occurring between the *uke* and the *nage*. This requires both the *uke* and the *nage* to have matured beyond the need to win, or have fear of failure. Both the *uke* and the *nage* can now enter the next stage of their training, where it is permissible for the *uke* to counter the *nage's* technique if execution of his/her defence offers a legitimate opening. *(However, it is imperative that the uke offers an honest attack in the first place—and maintains his/her intention to attack—at the prescribed speed based on the skill level of all participants.)*

Once the basics are understood and can be applied *(even at a slow pace)* against strong resistance, the training can progress into a much more dynamic and creative phase of the art, where no two situations are the same, and where all ego and attachment to winning must be dropped. At this skill level, new techniques are *"created"* under the inspiration of the moment as required in order to meet the challenge of single or multiple armed or unarmed attackers. This level of ability is referred to as *"TAKEMUSU AI-KI."* At this level of training the attitude of the *nage* must be totally noncompetitive, and he or she must remain calm and attentive to what is occurring all around—*moment to moment*—as if it were a game or challenge where physical technique and mental skill levels are being tested in order to discover both strengths and weaknesses in the person's ability to perform naturally while being subjected to increasing amounts of pressure. The contest is, therefore, actually occurring within you—with the *uke(s)* providing the necessary pressure—appropriate to the *nage's* skill level—in order for him or her to be able to discover where he or she needs to improve. Deep gratitude and respect result from this type of enlightened interaction. The intention is growth and development as opposed to the frustration and disappointment of competition, where the only intention is to decide a winner and a loser.

Free to train—as opposed to contend—the joy of continuous growth and self-discovery replaces the frustration and anger that accompanies the struggle to prove that you are better than others. In addition, fast training at too early a stage in your development is counterproductive to in-depth study and analysis of the many facets and fundamental principles that are at play in the dynamic interaction between the *uke* and the *nage*—things (at a basic level) such as effective and efficient movement, correct breathing, and balance and control of your mind. Incorrect training only binds you more and more to your fragile ego, and to the emotional turmoil that comes from desperately trying to maintain the illusion of superiority and control. Another very important consideration must be understood. Prematurely training in a fast manner will also result in the participants doing little more than skillfully "dancing" a choreographed performance where the attacker simply falls down in response to some preconceived understanding of his or her role in the martial interaction. This form of choreography has the potential to fuel your ego by making the martial interaction look legitimate when in fact all the *uke* is doing is attacking without any intent to win. To the uninformed observer the demonstration might look impressive; however, a skilled person will easily recognize ineffective martial interaction as the simple play of two people who have yet to progress beyond a mere superficial understanding of their art. The teacher understands that real fighting is ugly. The dynamic and devastatingly effective martial-arts techniques developed and refined over millennia are at the same time deadly yet extraordinarily alive because the movements are always spontaneous, vibrant, and alive with possibility.

Some advanced *martial-arts* techniques require you to step into your opponent's space while performing a self-defence technique, causing your partner to spiral up around you and unravel head first into the ground. This advanced skill requires that you fully accept the committed attack of your training partner, who doesn't necessarily know what your defence technique will be or even what his or her response to it will be. This, in turn, lays the foundation for a growing understanding of higher martial-arts principles.

When you observe a masterful execution of a martial-art technique, it's like being witness to something very, very special—something indefinable, something graceful, something harmonious, something beautiful, and yet something so explosively spontaneous and dangerous that it captures your imagination. The soul's yearning for self-realisation instantly recognizes the divine spirit that dwells within each one of us, and was glimpsed in the dynamic interaction between the *uke* and the *nage* because this is the true essence of *budō*.

The universe is matter and energy that are interacting harmoniously, and at peak efficiency, based on the universal laws and principles that govern our existence. These principles propagate life, and enable all parts of the whole to maintain an equilibrium that sustains all innate and living matter. It is the great *"dance of life,"* and the evolution of consciousness that we collectively call *the universe. Budō* is a way to attain a measure of alignment with this *"dance"* and with the evolution of consciousness. In fact, all great martial and yogic disciplines that espouse the *"Tao"*—or the *"way"* or a *"path"* to enlightenment—seek to express this understanding. Martial arts are, therefore, not simply an effective method of contention for the sake of victory—as *yoga* is not simply a method for increasing flexibility and improving health. Both actually offer you another dimension of possibility, a new paradigm that is actually a realisation of your original, unadulterated condition. Your training, therefore, aligns you with the natural *dance* of all of existence. This is the objective of all *Zen* arts that attempt to merge with the whole, and thereby—released from your isolated sense of self/selfishness—you gain everything in return.

"If all you think about is winning you will in fact lose everything. Know that you and your opponents are treading the same path."

—Morihei Ueshiba

10.0 Advanced Practices
10.1
Prana - Chi - Ki
10.2
Mind & Body Connection

10.1 Prâna-*Chi*-Ki

*"**Prâna**"* (from Indian philosophy), or *"**chi**"* (from Chinese philosophy), or *"**ki**"* (from Japanese philosophy) is used to describe an all-encompassing, universal *"life force" or "energy"* that exists throughout the universe. For you, the four main sources of this subtle life-force energy (*prâna*) are breath, sleep, water, healthy food, and the power of a calm yet concentrated mind capable of sustaining its intention.

The Indian word ***prâna*** comes from two Sanskrit words, *"**pra,**"* meaning constant, and *"**Na,**"* meaning movement. Based on ancient yogic principles, correct breathing and the mental control practices that underpin your *budō* training help you to gradually free your mind and body from tension and enhance your ability to accumulate, retain, circulate, and direct *prâna* throughout your body.

Learning to infuse your grounded, centred, spiraling physical movements with your breath, together with a specific highly focused intention, is what the founder of *Aikido,* Morihei Ueshiba, called *"kokyu-ryoku"* (literally meaning *"breath power*"). He manifested the physical power of *"ki"* through his dynamic circular martial-arts techniques charged with this special breath and mental focus. In fact, *Aikido's* reputation as a sophisticated spiritual discipline is founded on its emphasis on the accumulation, retention, circulation, and direction of your body's *intrinsic internal energy* (known in Japan as *"ki"*) in order to facilitate and enhance higher awareness.

This *"energy"* or *"life force"* has been known to martial-arts and yoga masters for centuries because it has the proven ability to enhance combat effectiveness as well as promote health, vitality, and spiritual awareness.

In *budō,* "ki" is initially understood by a practical understanding of how your body maintains optimum health and energy levels. The spiritual facet of *ki* (***prâna***) is obtained from your connection with something greater than yourself—from *physical matter* to *energy* to *mind* to the ultimate source of the *Absolute*. The conceptualization of this understanding outside of personal realisation is futile; however, in the context of *budō,* breath and mind are utilized to accumulate, store, and circulate *prâna or ki* throughout the body for enhanced health as well as physical performance and power.

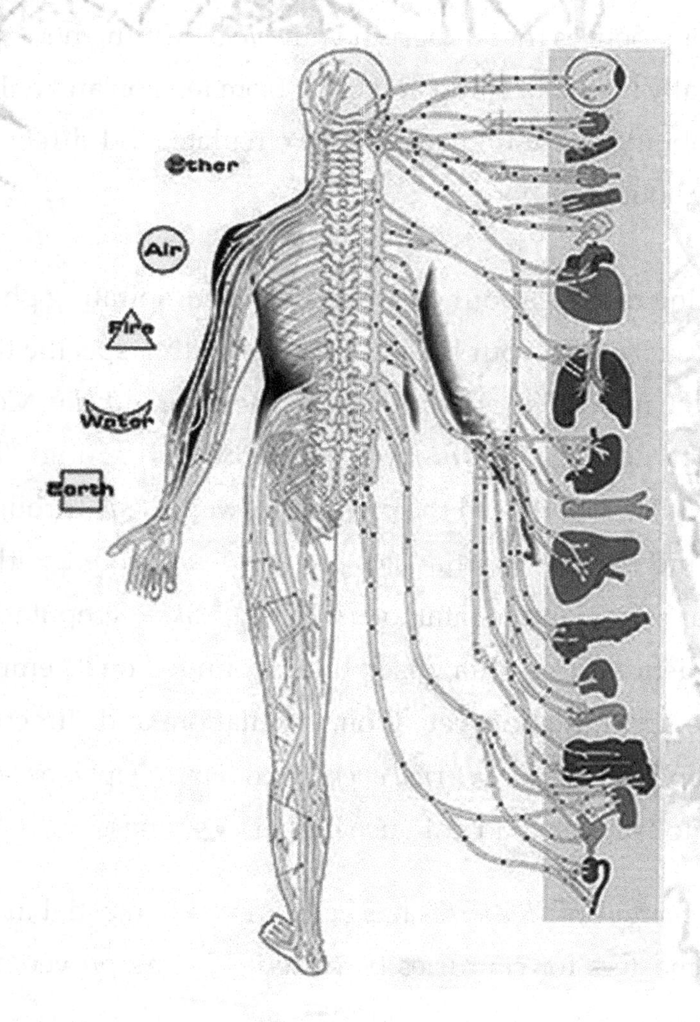

History of "Ki"

Chinese philosophers, attempting to interpret this Indian concept of *prâna,* defined it in many ways—including a metaphysical principle of duality that gives life, form, and structure to the universe (i.e., the concept of *yin* and *yang* by the Chinese philosopher Lao-tzu). The Chinese called their concept of *prâna "chi."* Acupuncture is also based on the fact that your health is dependent on the free-flowing circulation of *prâna,* or *chi,* throughout your body.

The introduction of the concept of *chi* from China into Japan saw the most dramatic changes in interpretation. Calling it ***"ki,"*** they translated it to mean several things, including power (*I-ki*), vigor (*gen-ki*), bravery (*yu-ki*), and breath control (*ki-soku*). The concept of *"prâna," "chi"* or *"ki,"* therefore, has a physical facet, as in breath, and optimum health and energy levels. It also has an emotional facet, as in state of mind. However, the single thread of spiritual understanding passed down from India to China and then to Japan was that this metaphysical concept of *prâna* (subsequently renamed and reinterpreted by China as *chi* and by Japan as *ki*) closely relates the life force within each person to a universal life force present in all of nature.

"Ki" and Spirituality

Based on how your five senses perceive the universe, it is easy to feel that you are a completely separate individual. But science is now affirming what the yoga sages have been telling us for thousands of years—that *prâna*—the *"life force"* of the universe, is the foundation that underpins all material existence. Imperceptible though it may seem to the gross physical senses, it is the very fabric of life. It is, therefore, impossible for you to exist separate from or outside of the source of all creation.

"All the principles of heaven and earth are living inside you. Everything in heaven and earth breathes. Breath is the thread that ties creation together. When the myriad vibrations in the universe can be sensed the individual techniques of the Art of Peace are born."

—Morihei Ueshiba

10.0 Advanced Practices
10.1
Prana - Chi - Ki
10.2
Mind & Body Connection

10.2 Mind and Body Connection

The miracle of life pulsates in every living cell of your body. As you initially bring your awareness to your body, you become a student of this miracle. Your training in *budō* penetrates deeply into the mystery of this fantastic phenomenon called human existence. First and foremost, it is crucial that you begin the process of respecting and befriending your body. Once you start to listen to, decontaminate, and nourish your body, you begin to empower its innate intelligence, wisdom, and dormant life force. *The next important thing to recognize is that mind and body are not separate entities.* Mind exists in every cell of the human body. Mind, therefore, has a very real, direct, and immediate influence over the body, and vice versa. It is, therefore, necessary to tame and discipline the mind, because left to run as an immature, emotional master, it has the potential to destroy you.

"Training in budō penetrates deeply into the mystery of this fantastic phenomenon called human existence."

—Jules Aib

The human body, especially the human brain, has undergone a very special and dramatic evolution in form, structure, and ability. This evolutionary process, involving human intelligence and consciousness, is expanding and accelerating at an unprecedented pace. You possess some remarkable tools—an extraordinarily evolved body, a miraculous brain with a mind on the threshold of enlightenment, and a consciousness endowed with truly *creative power.* However knowledge of a thing is not the same as being able to do it. You must take personal accountability for your own liberation. You cannot abdicate this responsibility to anyone else. With discipline and practice of awareness, you have the capacity to go deeper into the subtle layers of your consciousness, and watch from there. The practice of *budō* supports this personal journey of self-discovery.

"The goal of budō training is to seek insight into some of life's most fundamental questions: Who are we? Where do we come from? And why is it important?"

—Jules Aib

Scientific research is essential to help progress your understanding of yourself, your planet, and your place in the universe. However, in order to answer the most basic, fundamental questions of human existence you need to go *beyond* the study of the known universe and return to its source. Like science, however, the challenge is not to blindly acceptance dogma, but to undertake a structured investigation and exploration based on personal inquiry and experience—with your faculties of intellect, common sense, and reason fully functioning.

Budō, therefore, does not teach or advocate any specific belief system or any dogma. The limitation of adopting an attitude of blind faith (which has led to the segregation of belief systems, nations, and people) has caused much harm and destruction. It's time for each and every one of us to awaken from our deep and profound slumber using our faculties of reason, awareness, and discernment.

Quantum physics outlines the principle that human consciousness affects that which it observes at the subatomic level. Science has also established that the human brain produces waves of electromagnetic energy, or brain waves, called alpha (14-25Hz), beta (7-14 Hz), theta (4-7 Hz), and delta (<4 Hz). Meditation, mantras, sound/vibration, colours, aroma therapy, body movement, kinesthetic experience, breathing, hypnoses and visualization, etc., are all tools employed to alter brain wave cycles in order to induce altered states of consciousness. The objective of all these practices can be thought of as trying to gradual "*thin*" the intermediary layers between the various layers of consciousness enough for you to be able to directly observe the phenomena of each. These different layers of human consciousness, or continuous streams of awareness, result in a broad spectrum of understanding of reality based on the level of awareness, attention, or consciousness you bring to the equation. This can range from a direct, personal experience of reality all the way through to delusion, illusion, and a profound sense of duality, individuality, and separation.

In *yoga,* the subtle layers of human consciousness are defined as functioning at the following levels:

— ***Jagrat*** (waking consciousness—both objective and subjective)

- *Swapna* (subconsciousness)
- *Sushupti* (superconsciousness)
- *Turiya* (cosmic-consciousness)

Yoga gradually moves you from *Jagrat* to *Turiya* consciousness. Your mortal existence is required in order to facilitate this unfolding of your consciousness. What is on the other side of this *"veil of reality"* is the truth about your existence, your relationship to the whole, and your creative role in its ongoing expansion and evolution.

The difficulty is that you have grown up in a world full of social, political, and moral conditioning, full of prejudges. When young you were like a sponge, absorbing everything that you were subjected to. You soaked up the contaminated stuff just as readily as you soaked up the truth. Your first task, by necessity, must, therefore, be one of *decontamination* and *self-purification*. Emotions such as jealousy, greed, hatred, and fear cannot accompany you on your spiritual journey. However, they must be laid to rest in appropriate ways. Not ignored. Not suppressed. The more you struggle, the more resistance you will encounter. So your best strategy is to simply stop struggling and rethink your approach. Any teaching that condemns any aspect of life—physical or emotional—is counterproductive to spiritual progress. Nothing should be renounced out of hand without careful examination. Everything is integral to your divine nature. You are not separate from the things you try to renounce. It is what makes you part of the whole. It is also dangerous to sweep things under the carpet, because no matter how much you "vacuum" or "scrub" the outer surface, the "stench" will eventually filter up through the fibers and make your "house" a very unpleasant place to live in. You only need to look within yourself, in silence, once free from the burden of judgment, obligation, fear, greed, resentment, guilt, anxiety, and ignorance about what is truly important.

Every individual possesses specific strengths and weaknesses. You must, therefore, patiently and methodically find out for yourself what works for you, and what does not. Spiritual progress is easy to identify; it is clearly visible in qualities such as gratitude, compassion, empathy, kindness, simplicity, and selfless service. *But take note, these are not things to be blindly accepted or mechanically adopted.* They are the flowers that burst into life as a natural result of a spiritual awakening based on a disciplined, methodical, scientific-based approach to authentic personal inquiry and experience.

This is what is offered to you with both *budō* and yoga training: wisdom and insight based on personal inquiry and experience. With correct training, disempowering and unproductive ways of thinking and behaving are exposed to the pure light of day. Once you become aware of the things that are holding you back, you become equipped with vastly superior ways of thinking, feeling, and behaving. In time, with patient practice, old and ineffective ways will fall from you naturally, one by one. Both *budō* and yoga are, therefore, methodical, scientifically based, repeatable approach to personal and spiritual discovery based on a structured approach to mind/body training, where wisdom and insight are grounded in personal inquiry and experience.

For thousands of years, meditation has been considered essential by those who truly aspire to progress along the path of self-discovery and self-mastery because it brings awareness of how your mind works. You initially start to develop the skill of staying in complete consciousness by becoming aware of your breathing and by turning your attention inward. With meditation, you become a student of the processes that occur with your own mind and body simply by remaining in complete silence, with complete awareness and consciousness.

"Move within, but do not move the way that fear makes you move"

—Rumi

With practice, you create integration and wholeness within yourself. With silent observation, you simply watch how you create your own thoughts or emotions, and how the energy created from your emotions and mental attitudes affects your entire physical and spiritual system. This detached observation empowers you with the freedom to choose whether to allow your thoughts and emotions to control you. You learn to distinguish what is really important—to see what is actually happening (i.e., reality) as opposed to the inferences, beliefs, attitudes, and emotional turmoil that you allow to control your life.

Within the dynamic and diverse fabric of human existence, all approaches to self-actualization are valid. No approach is superior, and each human being will fulfill his or her destiny by the method that is most palatable to individual character, temperament, socialization, and understanding based on education and experience. A hindrance to realizing the possibilities of your potential is intolerance—prejudice or judgment of other people and the methods they pursue individually or collectively to gain a better understanding and acceptance of their seemingly infinitesimal existence in an infinite universe.

At the highest levels of *budō* training, your relaxed physical and mental state resembles that of a person sitting in peaceful meditation. The difference is that this relaxed state of being is required to be maintained while you are being attacked. In *budō*, an attacker, therefore, actually enhances the process of your mental and spiritual development. In fact, the situation created by your training partner(s) is critical for your effective development. Without the psychological, mental, and physical challenge of your training partner, you have to rely on solo exercises, which do not offer you the instant tangible feedback necessary to accurately gauge your progress.

"Unite yourself to the Divine . . ."

—Morihei Ueshiba

In *budō*, if your technique is not performed with the correct integration of mind, body, and breath, then your training partner is either able to successfully execute the attack against you or put up resistance to any attempt by you to control his/her aggression. However, if you perform the *martial-arts* technique with the correct spirit, your attackers are helplessly swept up, while your mind remains calm—centred in the *"eye of the storm."*

If executed with a nonviolent mindset, a kind of dynamic balance is experienced between you and your training partners. The attack is instantly neutralized with minimal physical effort and without struggle. This ability is a direct result of your being able to transcend your primary awareness beyond your ego, and slowly facilitates a growing realization of a connection between yourself and your training partners. Once this is truly experienced, gratitude, great joy, and love permeate your being.

"Ultimately you must forget about technique.
The further you progress the fewer teachings there are.
The Great Path is really No Path."

—Morihei Ueshiba

Man has devised many names to describe this experience. Great sages throughout history have attempted to point the way by use of symbols, allegory, poetry, art, music, and movement. They have also devised many disciplines that offer a path to enlightenment. The universal requirements of all methods are courage, determination, patience, and persistence. The universal rewards of such effort are self-knowledge, compassion, wisdom, and a fathomless wellspring of joy that naturally emerges from deep within the core of your being. You begin to live with complete integrity and complete honesty. Authenticity, selfless service, and a healthy lifestyle characterize a life strengthened by the power of contemplation, introspection, and meditation.

"You cannot see or touch the Divine with your gross senses. The Divine is within you, not somewhere else."

—*Morihei Ueshiba*

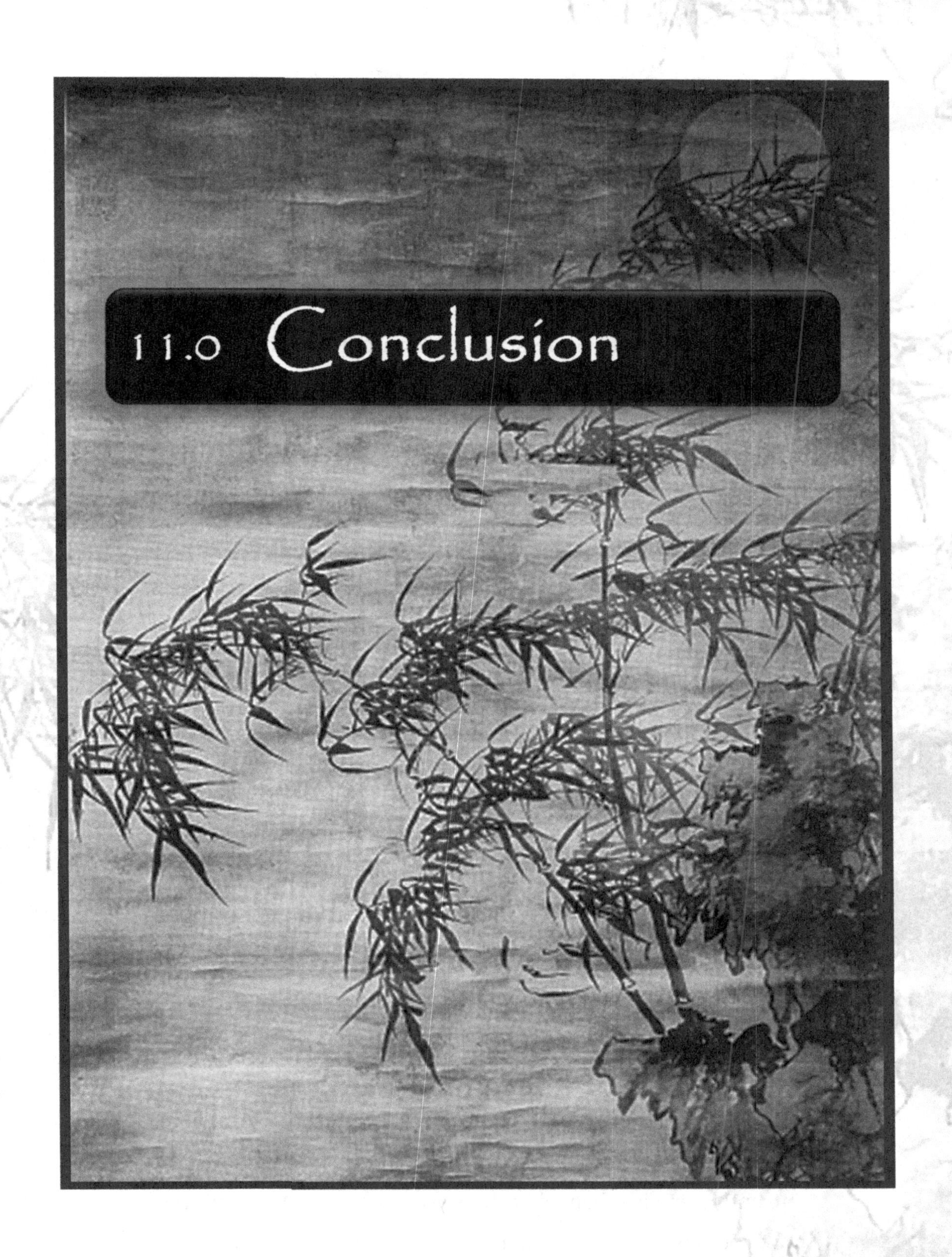
11.0 Conclusion

11.0 Conclusion

The *science of combat strategy* is relative. A strategy that is good for you may not be good for another. What is good at one time may not be good at another time and in another place. *Combat strategy* is, therefore, relative to an individual and his or her surroundings.

Just an intellectual understanding of a particular strategy is simply not enough to be effective or even useful. You must become disciplined enough to put the theory into practice in as many different situations as possible. Your goal of mastery should be underpinned by an attitude of never-ending, continuous improvement.

Therefore, in order to progress, you must do the simplest thing . . . and yet the hardest thing—you must remain totally vigilant and maintain a childlike quality about your training. Your ego, however, does not give up that easily. Even after many years of training you can still fall into the trap of complacency and stop paying close attention to what's happening in your head. Without continually cultivating a beginner's mind, where infinite possibilities always exist, you can get trapped in an "expert's" world, where you constantly make judgments about the *"right"* way and *"wrong"* way of doings things. *This mentality severely limits your possibilities.*

A *"beginner's mind"* is empowered to just be present—to explore, observe, and see things as they really are instead of how you currently perceive them to be, how you want them to be, or even how you would like them to be. The Japanese refer to this state of mind that remains ever alert, open, and aware as *"hoshin."* It is a state of awareness where you are always prepared to see things as if for the first time in order to continually gain deeper and deeper insight, understanding, and practical application. Therefore, based on this attitude, you are encouraged to be comfortable with not knowing everything and continue to search with the curiosity and wonder of a child at play. This also directly implies that the accountability for learning and growth rests squarely on your shoulders. You must, therefore, *"steal"* each technique from your teacher and weave the principles of the art into authentic personal experience. This ancient and time-tested approach to authentic personal self-discovery taps you into a wellspring of collective knowledge and wisdom that pours forth from this inquiring, fresh, and vital state of being that is referred to as *"beginner's mind."*

Everyone is different, so while studying the various combat strategies contained within this book, you need to ascertain which strategies best resonate with your personality out of all the strategies covered. Then, instead of just dabbling on the surface of each strategy, choose one or two to initially focus on before expanding your repertoire. It is all about the journey. Every day is a new day to learn and grow. Therefore, every day is a new day to deepen your understanding and to fail and retry in a never-ending process of discovery and skill refinement. You may move from one strategy to the other depending on your current technical skill level, but this systematic method of practice will curtail your desire to try to perfect everything all at once and will set you on a balanced path of true self-mastery. There should never come a day when you say *"I've finally got it,"* because if you do, then that is the moment when your progress will stop. By simply focusing on being better than you were yesterday, and aligning every moment of your life to your true purpose, you will automatically be on the right track. If you progress in this fashion, then you will be keeping it real, because the reality is that it has never been about the destination—*in reality, there is no ultimate destination.* Your objective is to die still learning and still growing. If you have trained properly, the last thought you will have in the twilight years of your life will still resonate with the awe, wonder, and curiosity that drove you to explore, practice, and grow in the first place. Then, at the inevitable end of your mortal journey, only three important questions will be left for you to answer:

1. What have you done that is sufficient?
2. What have you learnt?
3. Who have you loved?

Always hold this simple truth close to your heart: ***Your time here is brief***—so right now it's time for you to stop reading to gain *knowledge* and start training in order to gain *understanding.* There is no time to waste and no time like the present, *so start training!*

Jules Aib
Founder of World Aikido-Yoga (WAY)

About the Author

Mr. Jules Aib has studied martial arts and Eastern philosophy for almost four decades. His *Aikido* lineage can be traced back to the founder of *Aikido* through the late *Morihiro Saito Sensei* (1928-2002), who trained with the founder of *Aikido, Morihei Ueshiba* (1883-1969) for twenty-four years during the vital post-World War II evolution of *Aikido* in Iwama, Japan. *Saito Sensei* was a true modern master who devoted his life to the unadulterated dissemination of the founder's teachings. Prior to commencing his *Aikido* training, *Jules* applied himself to the study of *Shotokan Karate* under the late *Paul Guerillot Sensei* (1930-95), an innovative *budō* master who combined savat, karate, and knife-fighting techniques to create a system that he called foot and fist boxing. In more recent years Jules has embraced Brazilian Jiu-Jitsu (Founded by the late, great Hélio Gracie 1913–2009, a consummate martial arts master and role model who's legacy has influenced all aspects of modern mixed martial arts). Jules also undertook an intense study of *yoga* under the private tuition of *Javad Khansalar,* a modern yoga master, in India over a number of years. Upon his return to Australia from India in 1997 Jules founded World Aikido-Yoga (WAY) and continues to practice and teach the martial art of *Aikido-Yoga* around the world.

END

—"***Love***" *calligraphy by*
Morihei Ueshiba

Acknowledgments

First I would like to acknowledge some of the people who have stayed with me through "thick and thin" on my *Aikido-Yoga* journey—my second family: Thimmaiah M.C, chief instructor of *Aikido-Yoga* in India, who has been with me from the very beginning, along with Khader Ali Khan, Balaji B.K, Rob Watmuff, Irene Metter, Daniel Sharp, Amita Dottori, Daniel Somerville, Rick Pian, James Erving, Etsuko Yasunaga, Kieran and Jessica Gourley, Alon Kassir, Andrew Leech, Darryl Dillon-Shallard, Lee Stratton, Michael Smith, Maria John, David Bowman, Thomas Bowman, and last, but by no means least, Vanessa Ernst.

To my many, many *Aikido-Yoga* students and training partners over the years too numerous to mention—you know who you are. Even if you are no longer training, each one of you has enabled me to grow. *Thank you.*

To Protima Gauri Bedi, Surupa Sen, Bijayini Satpathy, Parvitra Reddy, and everyone at the Nrityagram Dance Village in Bangalore, India—*my sisters.*

To the many teachers who inspired the direction of my *Aikido-Yoga* journey, in particular, Javad Khansalar, Morihei Ueshiba, Morhiro Saito, Paul Guerillot, and Stephen R. Covey—your unique contributions will continue to spread throughout the world forever.

To Susanne, my darling wife and love of my life—*till death do us part.*

To Jonathan Aib and Olivia Aib—*You are the best of Susanne and me.*

And last, but not least—Mum, Dad, and Edith—*my blood.*

You have all contributed to the expansion of my heart . . .

Thank you also to all who contributed to making the historic photographs and illustrations in this book possible—your contribution to Aikido is special and very much appreciated. Special thanks to Irene Metter for her input to the cover design and Waseem Khan for the portrait photography of Jules Aib on pages IX, 143 and 249.

[illegible]

[illegible] and love my life [illegible]

[illegible]

[illegible]

[illegible]

[illegible]